Elementary Grade Two

Our Prophet Muhammad
TEXT BOOK

Salla Allahu alaihi wa sallam

Life in Makkah

Abidullah Al-Ansari Ghazi
Saba Ghazi Ameen

 IQRA' International Educational Foundation

Part of a Comprehensive, Integrated and Systematic Program of Islamic Studies

A Textbook for the Program of Sirah
Elementary Level Grade-2

Our Prophet: Textbook: part one

Chief Program Editors
Abidullah al-Ansari Ghazi
Ph.D. Harvard University
Tasneema Ghazi
Ph.D. University of Minnesota

Language Editors
Huseyin Abiba
Dilshad Ali

Art Work
Saba Ghazi Ameen

Design
Saba Ghazi Ameen

**Production
Coordinator**
Aliuddin Khaja

First printed in April, 2008
Printed in Singapore

Library of Congress Control Number: 2008925591
ISBN # 1-56316-182-6

IQRA'S Note

As-Salamu 'Alaikum!

Welcome to the new, revised and expanded edition of a Muslim children's classic textbook, Our Prophet Muhammad Rasulullah - Life in Makkah. We at IQRA' are very proud of the book's informative content and the high quality of graphics and illustrations, all of which was designed to convey the Sirah of our dear Prophet ﷺ to young minds and hearts.

The scholars and educators at IQRA' passionately believe that the total life story of Rasulullah ﷺ, as a whole, must be communicated to students sequentially and not in bits and pieces, shuffled into a single textbook with diverse subjects of Islamic religious knowledge. This work is a labor of love in which we have attempted to bring the Sirah closer to the hearts and minds of young Muslims so that they learn about the Mercy sent to Creation ﷺ, come to love him and then begin to emulate his perfected model. This textbook is a part of IQRA's systematic and comprehensive program of Islamic education, a program that has shaped a top-quality integrated educational system for the Islamic schools in North America and other parts of the English-speaking world. Our syllabi are designed to facilitate the teaching of the Islamic knowledge within a cross-curricular setting making use of the contemporary technology and critical thinking skills in the teaching and learning process.

Our Prophet Muhammad Rasulullah ﷺ - Life in Makkah introduces the basic pre-Hijra biography of Rasulullah ﷺ at a level of understanding that is aimed at 7 to 8 year-olds. The authors and designers have made special efforts to help young readers feel close to the Prophet ﷺ, energizing their love for him and encouraging them to follow in his footsteps. Therefore the textbook has been written in the uncomplicated and lucid language of a second grade reading level. The readability level of the text has been carefully evaluated to suit beginning readers. It is hoped, insha'Allah, that students will be able to grasp the concepts introduced in each lesson and adopt its teachings to every day life.

It is recommended that teachers use the accompanying workbook in conjunction with the textbook in the course of the class. The workbook has been prepared to provide pupils with important exercises in comprehension as well to aid in the development of critical thinking skills.

We invite you to join hands in our efforts by sending us your comments and suggestions. Let's begin to build a viable and expert program of Islamic education for our future generations!

Chief Editors

About the Book

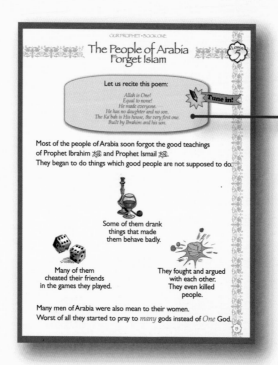

Tune in
- A brief focused introduction to the lesson.

Think about it
- Opportunities to think critically and discuss the lesson.

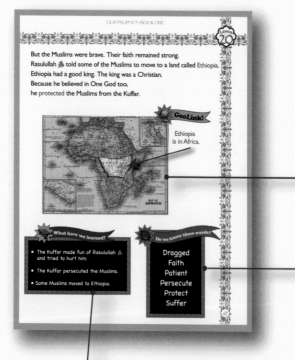

Geo Link
- Maps and description of physical and social geograph of a region, country or a city.

Do we know these words?
- List of new vocabulary words learned in the lesson

What we have learned?
- Review and recall of the basic concepts discussed in the lesson.

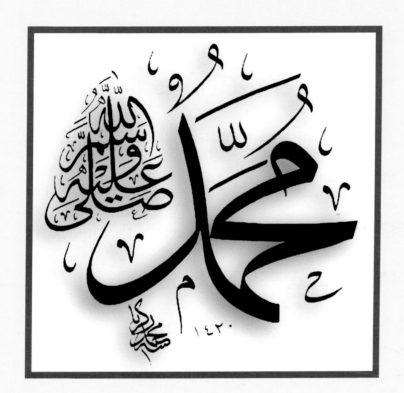

The publication of this book was made possible through a donation from the family of the late Saiema Mansoor with the intention of Isal Ath-Thawab (إيصال الثواب) for her.

Please remember her and all the believers in your Du‘a’.

Table of Contents

Table of Contents

Lesson 1 — Allah's Messenger

لا إله إلا الله محمّد رسول الله

"There is no god but Allah and Muhammad is the Messenger of Allah."

Do you know how many people around the world say these verses and believe in them?
Who is Allah? Who is Muhammad ﷺ?

Let us find out!

We are Muslims *al-Hamdulillah!*
Our religion is Islam.
Al-Hamdulillah means "All praises are for Allah".

الحمد لله

We believe that there is no god but Allah ﷻ.
Allah loves us. He wants us to be good.
We believe that Muhammad ﷺ is *Rasulullah*.
Rasulullah means Allah's Messenger.
We believe that Muhammad ﷺ is *Nabi-ullah* too.
Let us say it in Arabic:

لا إله إلا الله
La ilaha il Allah,

محمّد رسول الله
Muhammadun Rasulullah

The word Islam comes from the Arabic word *salima*, which means peace.
Islam is a religion of peace.
The word Islam also comes from another Arabic word *aslama*, which means to obey.
A Muslim obeys Allah and lives in peace.

Lesson 1

Allah sent many messengers and prophets to people.

Some of them we know.

Many more we do not know.

We believe in all of them.

The first prophet is Prophet Adam ﷺ.

The last prophet is Prophet Muhammad ﷺ.

Allah will not send any more prophets after Muhammad ﷺ.

Muhammad ﷺ is our prophet.

We are his *Ummah.*

Ummah means "people" or "nation."

An *Ummah* is a group of people who have the same beliefs.

We believe that Allah is the only God.

We believe that Muhammad ﷺ is Rasulullah.

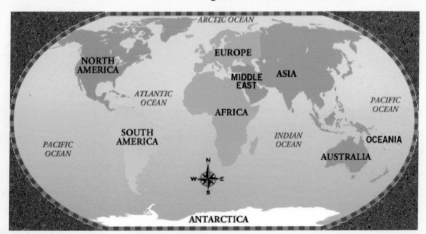

Allah ﷻ gave Rasulullah ﷺ the *Qur'an.*

The *Qur'an* is Allah's message to the people of the world.

The *Qur'an* is Allah's last message.

The *Qur'an* is for all times to come.

We write after the name of Allah ﷻ.

It means "The Praised and The Highest."
It reminds us to always remember
that Allah is Glorious and Great.

Rasulullah ﷺ loves his *Ummah*.
He always prayed for his *Ummah*.
On the Day of Judgment Allah will answer his prayers.

The *Ummah* of Rasulullah ﷺ loves him.
They want to follow his *Sunnah*.
Sunnah means his teachings and his actions.

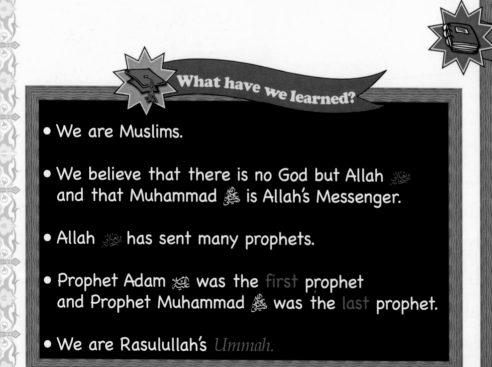

What have we learned?

- We are Muslims.

- We believe that there is no God but Allah ﷻ and that Muhammad ﷺ is Allah's Messenger.

- Allah ﷻ has sent many prophets.

- Prophet Adam ﷺ was the first prophet and Prophet Muhammad ﷺ was the last prophet.

- We are Rasulullah's *Ummah*.

Do we know these words?

Praise
Believe
Messenger
Ummah
Obey
Nabi-ullah

We Love Our Prophet ﷺ

Tune in!

Let us recite the verses below
in praise of our dear Prophet Muhammad ﷺ!

بلغ العلا بكماله
Balagh al-Ula bi Kamalihi

كشف الدّجى بجماله
Kashafad Duja bi Jamalihi

حسنت جميع خصاله
Hasunat Jam'iu Khisalihi

صلّوا عليه وآله
Sallu Alaihi wa Alihi!

"He reached the highest level of perfection
He lifted the darkness with his beauty
Tremendous are his traits
Send blessings upon him and his family!"

All Muslims love Rasulullah ﷺ.
He is our prophet.

He is Allah's last prophet.
He was good and kind to everyone.
He was fair and loving to everyone.

Rasulullah ﷺ loved everyone.
He told us to do what is good.
We should do what he told us to do.

When we follow Rasulullah ﷺ we are following Allah ﷻ.
Allah ﷻ will be happy with us.
Allah ﷻ will take care of us in this life.
He will take care of us in the next life.
Once *A'ishah* ؓ, the Prophet's wife,
was asked by a companion of the beloved Messenger ﷺ,

> *"Tell me about the character of Muhammad ﷺ?"*

She instantly replied,

> *"You ask of the character of Muhammad?*
> *Indeed his character is the Qur'an."*

Whenever we hear Rasulullah's name we should say,

"Salla Allahu alaihi wa sallam."

This means, "May Allah's blessings and peace be upon him."

We write ﷺ after Rasulullah's name.
This means, *"Salla Allahu alaihi wa sallam."*
This reminds us to ask Allah ﷻ to bless Rasulullah ﷺ.

Allah ﷻ is happy with those people who say
"Salla Allahu alaihi wa sallam" after Rasulullah's name.

Allah ﷻ I tells us in the Qur'an that:
"Allah and His angels send their salutation on the Prophet, O believers, send your salutation on him and offer your Salam."

(al-Ahzab:56)

Rasulullah ﷺ said,
"He is real stingy who hears my name and does not send Salawat upon me".

Allah ﷻ and His angels bless us when we send *Salawat* on Rasulullah ﷺ.

In this book, we will read about the life of Rasulullah ﷺ. We will also read some of his sayings.

Rasulullah's sayings are called *Ahadith*. We need to learn the *Ahadith* and follow them.

We need to follow our dear Rasulullah ﷺ.

What have we learned?

- When we hear Rasulullah's name we should say: *"Salla Allahu alaihi wa Sallam"*

- We should love and obey our prophet Muhammad Rasulullah ﷺ.

- We should learn the Ahadith.

- We should follow the Ahadith.

Do we know these words?

Love

Ahadith

obey

Salla Allahu-
alaihi wa Sallam

Salawat

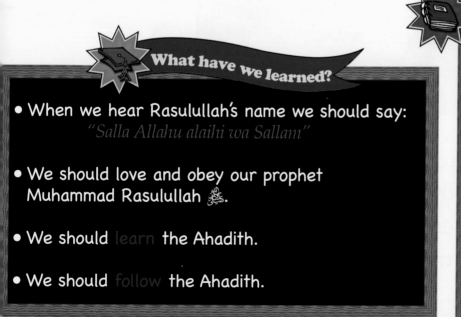

Lesson 3

The Arabian Peninsula

Tune in!

Look at the map of the world below.
Can you recognize the land called the Arabian Peninsula?

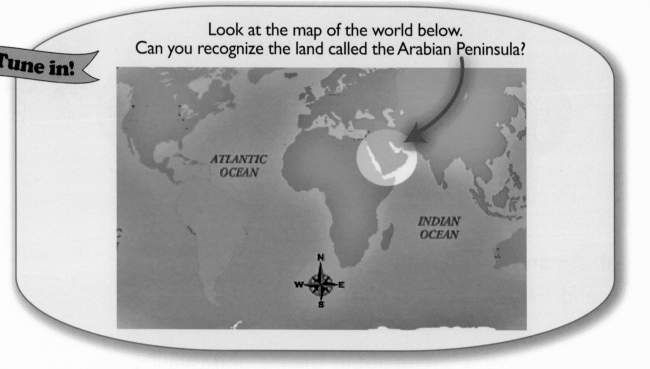

The Arabian Peninsula touches two big seas:

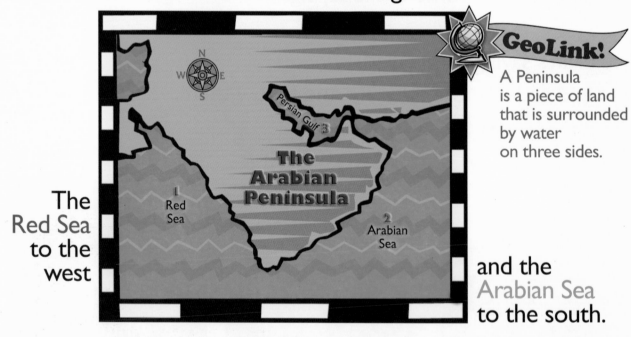

GeoLink!

A Peninsula is a piece of land that is surrounded by water on three sides.

The Red Sea to the west

and the Arabian Sea to the south.

The Persian Gulf is to the east.

Many people travel these seas on boats.

The Arab people used to sail on boats in these seas during the time of Rasulullah ﷺ

The two most special cities for Muslims are Makkah and Madinah.
They are in a country now called Saudi Arabia. Can you find them?

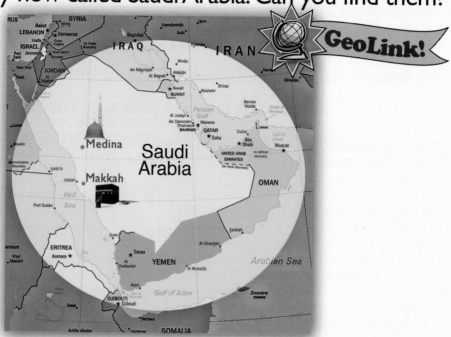

Most of Saudi Arabia is hot and dry.
A desert covers most of the land.
A desert is a place that is hot and very dry.
It rarely rains in a desert.

The first House of Allah,
the Ka'bah, is in Makkah.
Rasulullah ﷺ was born in Makkah.
Allah ﷻ sent the first Ayahs
of the Qur'an in Makkah.

We go to Makkah to make the Hajj.
The Hajj is a special pilgrimage.

Lesson 3

The city of Madinah is very special.
It is called *Madinat un-Nabi,* the "City of the Prophet."

The people of Madinah helped Rasulullah ﷺ.
Rasulullah ﷺ lived the last 10 years of his life in Madinah.

He built the Masjid Nabi in Madinah.
He is buried in Madinah.

We travel to Madinah to make *Salawa*
on our dear Prophet Muhammad ﷺ.

We pray in the Masjid of our Prophet ﷺ

What have we learned?

- Prophet Muhammad ﷺ was born in Makkah.

- The city of Makkah is in Arabia.

- Prophet Muhammad ﷺ received the first Ayahs of the Qur'an in Makkah.

- Most of Arabia is a desert.

- Arabia is surrounded by three bodies of water: the Red Sea, Arabian Sea and the Persian Gulf.

- The Masjid of the Prophet ﷺ is in Madinah.

Do we know these words

Desert
Arabia
Persian Gulf
Peninsula
Ayahs
Tawwaf
Hajj
Salawat

Prophet Ibrahim ﷺ &
Prophet Isma'il ﷺ Teach Islam

Lesson
4

Tune in!

"And remember when Ibrahim and Isma'il were raising the foundation of the House, (praying to Allah): 'Our Lord! Accept this service from us. Truly, you are the All-Hearer, and All-Knower.'"
(al-Baqarah:128)

Prophet Ibrahim ﷺ is called *Khalilullah,* the "Friend of Allah."

A long time before Rasulullah was born, Prophet Ibrahim ﷺ came to a deserted place called Makkah.
There was no city back then. It was an empty valley between rocky mountains.

Allah ﷻ asked Prophet Ibrahim ﷺ to leave his wife, Hajar ﵂, and their baby son, Isma'il ﷺ in Makkaha. But Allah took care of baby Isma'il ﷺ and his mother. He gave them fresh water from the Well of Zamzam.

Hajra ﵂ and her baby were the first people to live in Makkah. Some Arab tribes later came to the Valley of Makkah. They asked Hajar's permission to live there. She was very happy to have some neighbors.

Lesson 4

She invited them to live in Makkah.
This is how the city of Makkah was established.

The people lived in their tents.
The only place where they could get water
was from the Well of Zamzam.

Years later Allah ﷾ asked Prophet Ibrahim ﷺ
to build the *Ka'bah*.
He told Prophet Ibrahim ﷺ that the *Ka'bah*
would become a special place.

Isma'il ﷺ was a
young man then.
He helped his father
to build the *Ka'bah*.
They built the *Ka'bah*
so people could pray
to Allah there.

Prophet Ibrahim ﷺ loved Allah ﷾ very much.
Allah ﷾ made him a prophet and taught him Islam.
Prophet Ibrahim ﷺ then taught Islam to the people.

Islam teaches:

- There is only one God: Allah ﷻ.
- Allah created everything.
- No one is like Him.
- No one shares His power.
- He has no partners.
- He has no sons or daughters.

Prophet Ibrahim عليه السلام and Prophet Isma'il عليه السلام told the people that:

We should not worship or pray to false gods

We should obey Allah ﷻ.

We should be good to other people.

We should not be mean to them

After a while, people forgot these teachings.
They started to believe that:

- There were many gods besides Allah ﷻ.
- They believed that some of those gods were Allah's sons and daughters.
- They believed that many gods shared Allah's powers.

These beliefs were not right.
The people who believed in them had left Allah's religion.
They had turned away from Him.

Lesson 4

The Story of Zamzam

Prophet Ibrahim ﷺ took his wife Hajar and baby son Isma'il ﷺ to the Valley of Makkah in Arabia. It was a long journey. When they came to the valley, Prophet Ibrahim ﷺ spent some time with his wife and son. Then he told Hajar ﷺ that he had to go back to where they came from and leave her with the baby. Hajar ﷺ was afraid at first, but Prophet Ibrahim ﷺ told her that this was the Will of Allah ﷻ. She put her faith and trust in Allah ﷻ. She sat alone in the valley and nursed her baby. Soon there was no more water and no milk in her for the baby.

Hajar ﷺ knew she must find water. She laid the baby down and began to look. She ran to the top of the hill called *Safa* and looked all around. There were no people and no water in sight. Then she ran across the hot desert sand to the top of another hill called *Marwa*. She looked and looked but there was nothing to be seen. She ran back and forth seven times between the two hills. The entire time she was praying to Allah ﷻ for help.

Then Hajar ﷺ looked back at baby Isma'il ﷺ and saw a miracle. An Angel hit the earth with its wing right next to the baby. *Subhan Allah!* Water began to gush out of the sand! Hajar ﷺ ran back to the baby. She was so happy. She gave a drink to her thirsty baby and drank herself. Then she scooped up enough water with her hands to fill her water bag. Hajar ﷺ was so excited to find water in the desert. She did not want the water to flow into the sand. She began to dig the ground around the water to keep it from spilling over. She kept on saying, *"Zam! Zam!"* Which meant "Stop! Stop!" in her language. Since then the well is named Zamzam.

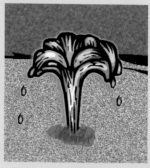

What have we learned?

- The Ka'bah was built by Prophet Ibrahim ﷺ and his son, Prophet Isma'il ﷺ.

- These prophets taught Islam to the people of Arabia.

- People forgot about Allah after the death of Ibrahim ﷺ and his son.

Do we know these words?

Build

Deserted

Pray

Worship

Religion

The People of Arabia Forget Islam

Recite this poem:

Allah is One!
Equal to none!
He made everyone.
He has no daughter and no son.
The Ka'bah is His house, the very first one.
Built by Ibrahim and his son.

Let us memorize it now

Tune in!

Most of the people of Arabia soon forgot the good teachings of Prophet Ibrahim and Prophet Ismail.
They began to do things which good people are not supposed to do.

Some of them drank things that made them behave badly.

They gambled and cheated their friends in the games they played.

They fought and argued with each other. They even killed innocent people.

Many men of Arabia were also mean to their women.
Worst of all they started to pray to *many* gods instead of *One* God.

Lesson 5

As Muslims, we pray only to Allah ﷻ. There are no other gods. Only Allah ﷻ is God. Allah ﷻ created everything. No one can do anything without His permission.

The people of Makkah began to put *idols* inside the Ka'bah. *Idols* are statues of different gods. They changed the Ka'bah from the House of the One God to the house of many gods. Allah ﷻ sent Rasulullah ﷺ as His last messenger to remind the people of Allah and Islam.

Belief in only One God ﷻ is called *Tawhid*.
This means that Allah ﷻ is the only Creator and Lord of the Universe.
No one is like Him.

Rasulullah ﷺ taught the people once again:

Allah is One
الأحد
Allah is One

• There is only one god, Allah ﷻ.
• Allah ﷻ created everything.
• No one is like Him.
• No one shares His power.
• He has no partners.
• He has no sons or daughters.

Rasulullah ﷺ told the people that:

We should be
good to everyone.

FOOD BANK

We should be ready
for our next life,
which will come after we die.

We should not
be mean to anyone.
We should help everyone.

What have we learned?

- Sometime after the death of Prophet Ibrahim and Isma'il ﷺ , people forgot their teachings.

- People began to pray to false gods.

- They made idols and prayed to them.

- They put idols in Ka'bah.

- Allah ﷻ sent Muhammad ﷺ as His last Prophet to teach people.

Do we know these words?

Idols
Behave
Cheat
Death
False

Lesson 5

Think about it!

Rewrite each group of words in order from:

smallest to largest:

City, Peninsula, Continent

....

first to last:

Christianity, Judaism, Islam

....

first to last:

Ibrahim ﷺ, Muhammad Rasulullah ﷺ, Adam ﷺ

....

most important to least important:

Hadith, Qur'an, a book of history

....

smallest to largest:

Family, *Ummah*, tribe

....

The Year of the Elephant

Have you heard the story
of the "People of the Elephant"
and about King Abraha who wanted to destroy the Ka'bah?

**Let us find out what happened
during the year when this event took place?**

After the death of Prophet Ibrahim ﷺ Makkah grew into a big town. People from all over Arabia came to Makkah to visit the Ka'bah. They came to pray to the idols that were inside it.

There was a land in the Arabian Peninsula called Yemen. One of the kings of that land was a man named Abraha.

He wanted the people to visit Yemen instead of Makkah. So he built a big temple in his land, but very few people visited his temple. That made him very angry.

Lesson
6

He made a plan to tear down the Ka'bah.
King Abraha called all his soldiers.
He told them they had to go to Makkah.
They marched through the desert.
They brought some big elephants.
They wanted to tear down the Ka'bah.

The people of Makkah were afraid of King Abraha.
They heard that his army was on the way.
They ran away from their homes.
They hid up in the mountains.

The family of Banu Hashim used
to take care of the Ka'bah.
Abdul-Muttalib was their leader.
He worried about the Ka'bah.
He knew he could not save it by himself. He prayed to Allah,

" Oh Allah! You are the owner of the Ka'bah.
We are weak. You are strong. You save it from Abraha!"

After many weeks Abraha's army arrived at Makkah. King Abraha told his army to attack. But something strange happened. The elephants in his army did not move. Their feet got stuck in the sand. The soldiers became afraid when they saw this.

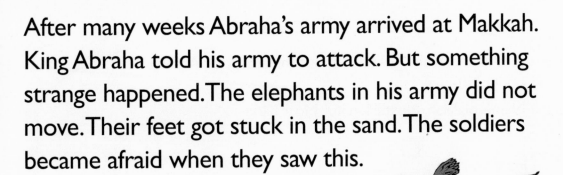

Then Allah ﷻ sent thousands of birds flying over Abraha's army. These birds dropped little rocks onto the soldiers. Some of his soldiers ran away. Most of them were completely destroyed. They never came back to Makkah. Allah ﷻ had protected the Ka'bah.

The people of Makkah came down from the mountains.

The Year of the Elephant

They were very happy. They called that year the Year of the Elephant.

This was the year when Prophet Muhammad ﷺ was born. Allah ﷻ sent him to teach people to believe in One God. Allah ﷻ sent him to teach people to live in peace.

Lesson 6

In the Qur'an, Allah ﷻ talks about the attack of Abraha. Let's read *Surah al-Fil*:

In the Name of Allah, Most Merciful, Most Kind

1

Have you not seen how your Lord dealt with the People of the Elephant?

2

Did He not make their evil plan fail?

3

And He sent against them flock of birds,

4

Striking them with stones of baked clay.

5

Then He made them like a crop that is chewed up.

What have we learned?

- Yemen is a land south of Saudi Arabia.

- Abraha was the king of Yemen.

- King Abraha wanted to tear down the Ka'bah.

- Allah has the power to stop anything.

- Abraha's army was destroyed.

- The Prophet Muhammad ﷺ was born in the Year of the Elephant.

Do we know these words

Visit
Surah al-Fil
Temple
Yemen
Protected
Destroy

The People of the Elephant

We read that King Abraha wanted
all the Arabs to go to Yemen to visit his temple.
He decided to attack Makkah and tear down the Ka'bah.
Use the chart below to make a timeline
of the events of King Abraha and his army
as they attacked Makkah

Beginning

▶ King Abraha and his army marched from Yemen to Makkah

Event 1

▶

Event 2

▶

Event 3

▶

End

▶ Allah ﷻ destroyed King Abraha and his army

Lesson 7 · The Birth of Muhammad Rasullullah

Tune in!

A Special Baby
It is said that Aminah ﷺ saw a light coming out of her.
The light told her that her baby would be a very "special person."
Who was this special baby?
Who was Aminah ﷺ?
Let's find out in this lesson!

Muhammad ﷺ was born in the Year of the Elephant.
He was born in the town of Makkah.

His father's name was Abdullah.
Abdullah's father was Abdul Muttalib.
Abdul Muttalib was one of the most important
men in Makkah. He took care of the Ka'bah.

Abdullah was a noble young man
from Makkah. He married a fine
young lady from Madinah.
The young lady's name was Aminah.

Abdullah and Aminah were very happy
together. They took care of each other.
They helped each other.

They took care of their parents.
They were kind to people.
They helped their neighbors.

They soon found out they were going to have a baby.
Allah ﷻ chose them to be very special parents.

Before the baby was born, 'Abdullah
had to travel to Madinah. It was a long
journey. While he was in Madinah he
got sick and died.

Aminah ﵐ was very sad after her husband died.
She prayed to Allah ﷻ to help her.
She prayed to Allah ﷻ to help her baby.

One night, Aminah ﵐ had a dream. In her dream,
she saw a light coming out of her. It made her
feel that her baby was a very special one.

Baby Muhammad ﷺ was born on the
12th Rabi al-Awwal. This is the third month
of Islamic Calendar. Aminah ﵐ was very happy
to see her baby boy. She prayed to Allah ﷻ
to make her baby grow into a noble man.

Rabi - ul Awal
12

Lesson 7

Aminah called for 'Abdul Muttalib, 'Abdullah's father. 'Abdul-Muttalib was very happy to know about the baby. He loved his new grandson very much.

'Abdul-Muttalib took the baby to the Ka'bah. There he thanked Allah ﷻ. He named the new baby "Muhammad." He also called him "Ahmad." This means *"someone who is praised by everybody."* 'Abdul-Muttalib wanted his grandson to be praised by Allah and by all the people on earth.

"Muhammad" means one "who is loved & praised by every one". It was a new name for the Makkans.

What have we learned?

- Rasulullah ﷺ was born in the year when Abraha attacked Makkah.

- His father's name was Abdullah. His mother was Aminah.

- Abdullah died before the Prophet ﷺ was born.

- Allah ﷻ sent many signs to Aminah about the special baby Muhammad ﷺ.

- Abdul-Muttalib was the grand father of Muhammad ﷺ.

- He named the baby Muhammad ﷺ.

Do we know these words:

Noble
Special
Attack
Signs

26

Little Muhammad ﷺ Lives with Halima ﷺ

A Life in the Village
Clear air, fresh food and
beautiful pure Arabic language!
Where can you find all of the above?

Let's find out in this lesson!

Tune in!

The rich families of Makkah liked to send their newborn babies to live in the countryside. The air was clean and fresh there.

The people living in the countryside. spoke pure Arabic.

Aminah ﷺ and Abdul Muttalib wanted to send baby Muhammad ﷺ to live with a family of villagers.

One day a woman from the tribe of Banu Sa'd came to Makkah. She wanted a baby that she could take back with her to her village. Her name was Halimah.

Aminah ﷺ and Abdul-Muttalib liked Halimah.
They found that Halimah ﷺ liked little baby Muhammad ﷺ.
They told her to take Muhammad ﷺ to her village
and raise him for two years.

Halimah and her husband were very happy.
Baby Muhammad was a blessed baby.
He brought a lot of *Barakah* to those around him.
Barakah means "Blessings."
Halimah's camel began to walk very fast.
Her goat began to give a lot of milk.

There was a drought in
the village of Banu Sa'd.

But when Halimah brought
baby Muhammad, it rained
and every one was happy.
The plants and vegetables
began to grow. Every one
told Halimah that Muhammad
was a special baby.

After two years had passed, Halimah asked Aminah
and Abdul Muttalib to let Muhammad stay in the village
for a few more years. Aminah agreed.
Muhammad stayed with Halimah for two more years.
He grew into a strong and healthy boy.

What have we learned?

- The rich Arab families of Makkah used to send their babies to be raised by villagers who spoke pure Arabic.

- Muhammad ﷺ lived with Halima ◌ in the village of Banu Sa'd.

- He was a blessed baby.

- He brought a lot of Barakah to the village of Banu Sa'd.

Do we know these words?

Countryside
Village
Barakah
Drought
Banu Sa'd

Muhammad ﷺ as a Child

Tune in!

Allah ﷻ tells us in the Qur'an
to be kind to the orphans.
Muhammad ﷺ was an orphan.
Who are the orphans?
Let's find out in this lesson!

Muhammad ﷺ returned to his family from the
village of his foster mother, Halimah.
He then lived with his mother and grandfather.

Aminah ﭪ loved her son very much.
She took very good care of him.
He was happy to be home.
He was a very special boy.

Muhammad's father, Abdullah, died before he was born.
Little Muhammad ﷺ did not even see his father.

The Prophet Muhammad ﷺ said about orphans:

*"The best house among the Muslims
is the house in which orphans
are well treated.
The worst house among the Muslims
is the house in which orphans
are treated badly.
I and the guardian of the orphan
will be in the Garden like this"*

He put his two fingers close together as he explained.

Aminah ﷺ traveled to the town of Madinah with young Muhammad ﷺ.
She wanted him to visit the grave of his father Abdullah.
But on their way back Aminah ﷺ fell sick and died.

Muhammad ﷺ was now an orphan.
An orphan is a child whose mother and father have died.
Muhammad ﷺ was only six years old.
He was very sad.

Muhammad ﷺ went to live with his grandfather, Abdul Muttalib.
Abdul Muttalib took very good care of the boy.
He would take him every where he went.
He would never let Muhammad ﷺ out of his sight.

After two years, Abdul Muttalib also died.
Muhammad ﷺ was lonely again.
So Muhammad's uncle, Abu Talib, took care of him.

Lesson 9

Abu Talib was the brother of 'Abdullah.
Abu Talib loved Muhammad ﷺ and Muhammad loved him.
Abu Talib took very good care of his nephew.
Even though Abu Talib had eight children,
he loved Muhammad ﷺ like his own son.
Muhammad ﷺ loved to be with his cousins.

Everyone in Makkah liked Muhammad ﷺ .
He was a happy and friendly boy.
He always played nicely and helped other people.

When Muhammad ﷺ grew up,
people loved and trusted him.
He always told the truth.
He never told lies. The people of
Makkah called him *as-Sadiq.*

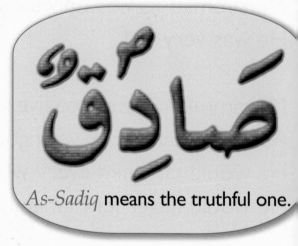

As-Sadiq means the truthful one.

Al-Amin means a person whom you can trust.

Muhammad ﷺ was very hones
fair and just. People felt safe to
leave things in his care.
The people of Makkah also
called him *al-Amin.*

Let us pray to Allah ﷻ to help us follow our dear Prophet ﷺ
Let us work hard to be honest and truthful.

What have we learned?

- Muhammad's ﷺ father, 'Abdullah died before he was born.

- His mother, Aminah died when he was six years old.

- Prophet Muhammad ﷺ lived with his grandfather for two years.

- His grandfather died when he was eight years old.

- After the death of his grandfather, Muhammad ﷺ lived with his uncle, Abu Talib.

- Everyone loved young Muhammad ﷺ. They called him *Al-Sadiq* and *Al-Amin.*

Do we know these words?

Orphan

Nephew

Friendly

Trust

Honest

As-Sadiq

Al-Amin

Muhammad ﷺ: a Merchant

Lesson 10

Tune in!

"Merchant, business people, traders"; these are the words used to describe people who buy and sell things.

It is *Sunnah* to be a business person. Why do you think it is a *Sunnah*?

Let's find out about it in this lesson!

Abu Talib was a merchant. He used to go on long business trips. He taught Muhammad ﷺ how to buy and sell things.

Soon Muhammad ﷺ became a merchant as well. Muhammad ﷺ liked helping his uncle in business.

Muhammad ﷺ was an honest merchant. People trusted him. They gave him their money to buy and sell things for them.

People thought that Muhammad ﷺ would become very rich one day.

But Allah ﷻ had other plans for Muhammad ﷺ.

When Muhammad ﷺ was a teenager, he went with
Abu Talib to visit the towns of Syria. In those days,
merchants used to travel in caravans. A caravan is a group
of people who travel together for protection.

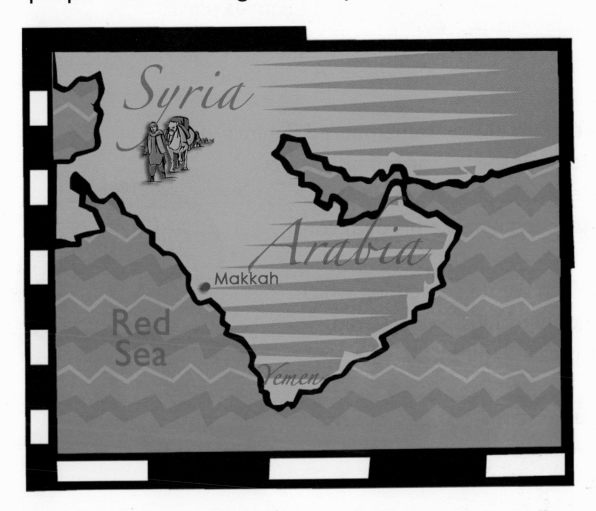

The caravan stopped to rest near one
of the towns of Syria. Abu Talib and
the other merchants set up their tents.
They set up their tents near the home
of a Christian monk named Bahira.
Bahira was a scholar and he read the
Injil and many other books.

Lesson
10

When Bahira saw the group he wanted
to talk to young Muhammad ﷺ.
After talking to him, Bahira said to Abu Talib,

*"Take good care of your nephew.
One day he will be a great prophet
and messenger of God."*

Abu Talib always remembered Bahira's words.
He took special care of his nephew.
He always protected him.
He loved him like his own son.

When we do something which
Prophet Muhammad ﷺ did,
it is called the *Sunnah.*

Business is a *Sunnah* of Prophet Muhammad ﷺ.
We should be fair and honest in our business.

When Rasulullah ﷺ was born, many people of the Middle East were Christians.

There were some special men and women
who dedicated their lives to their religion.
They would live in places far from other people,
like caves or huts. They did not want to be
bothered by other people. They only wanted
to study their religion and think about God.
These people were called monks.

What have we learned?

- Young Muhammad ﷺ used to go on business trips with his uncle Abu Talib.

- Once they met a Christian monk named Bahira, who told Abu Talib that Muhammad ﷺ would be a "great prophet and messenger of God."

- Muhammad ﷺ was an honest business man.

- Honest business is a Sunnah of Rasulullah ﷺ.

Do we know these words?

Merchant

Buy

Sell

Teenager

Caravan

Travel

Honest

Rich

Muhammad ﷺ and Khadijah ﷛ Marry

Tune in!

Love: A Sign Of Allah
"He has put love and Mercy between your hearts: Indeed that are signs for those who think"
(Surah 30:21)

Let us see how much prophet Muhammad ﷺ and Khadijah ﷛ loved each other

A noble lady named Khadijah ﷛ lived in Makkah. She was a widow. A widow is a lady whose husband has died. Khadijah was a rich business woman. She was beautiful and kind.

One day she asked Muhammad ﷺ to work for her. He took a caravan of goods to Syria for her. Muhammad ﷺ sold Khadijah's goods and bought other items. He came back with a lot of money. She was very happy with Muhammad ﷺ.

38

One day Khadijah ﷢ sent her servant,
Maisarah, to find out more about Muhammad ﷺ.
Maisarah told her how honest, kind and gentle he was.

Khadijah ﷢ liked his politeness and helpfulness.
Everyone who worked with Muhammad ﷺ
said that he was fair, honest and kind.
He never lied or cheated.

Muhammad ﷺ did very good work for Khadijah ﷢.
Her business made very good profit.
She was happy with Muhammad ﷺ.
She knew he was a good man.

One day Khadijah ﷢ asked
Muhammad ﷺ to marry her.
"Yes" he said, "You are a
good woman. I will marry you."

Muhammad ﷺ was 25 years old and Khadijah ﷢ was 40.
It was a happy marriage.

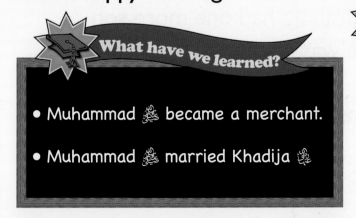

What have we learned?

- Muhammad ﷺ became a merchant.

- Muhammad ﷺ married Khadija ﷢

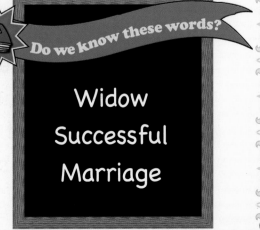

Do we know these words?

Widow
Successful
Marriage

Muhammad ﷺ and Khadijah's Children

 Tune in!

The Blessed Family
Some families are big and some are small.
Do you have a large family or a small one?
May Allah bless the family of Rasulullah ﷺ

Let us read more about the family of Rasulullah ﷺ and Khadijah.

Prophet Muhammad ﷺ and Khadijah
loved each other very much.
They were kind to each other.
They took care of each other.
They helped each other.

Muhammad ﷺ and Khadijah were very happy.
They had six children.
They had two sons and four daughters.

Their first child was a boy named Qasim.
Qasim became sick and died when he was two years old.
Everyone was sad.

Muhammad ﷺ and Khadijah had one more son.
But he also died when he was young.
His name was Tayyib.
Muhammad ﷺ and Khadijah became very sad
for the loss of their sons.

They thanked Allah for their daughters.
They named their daughters:
Zainab, Ruqayyah, Umm Kulthum and Fatimah.

Zainab 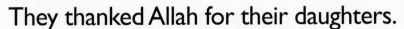 was the oldest and Fatimah 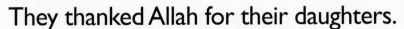 was the youngest.
Their parents took very good care of them.
They taught them good manners.
All of them grew up and became very good Muslimahs.

They loved their father and mother very much.
They always obeyed their parents.
They helped them in the housework.
They were kind to their neighbors.

Everyone liked the daughters of Muhammad ﷺ and Khadijah رضى الله عنها. May Allah bless the children of Prophet Muhammad ﷺ.

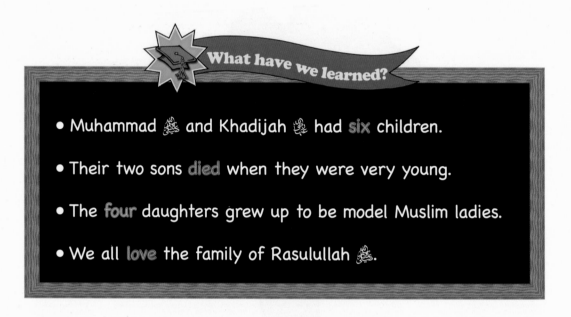

What have we learned?

- Muhammad ﷺ and Khadijah رضى had six children.

- Their two sons died when they were very young.

- The four daughters grew up to be model Muslim ladies.

- We all love the family of Rasulullah ﷺ.

Do we know these words?

Children

Daughters

Sons

Young

GUESS WHO?

Read each passage about Prophet Muhammad's family.
Can you guess which family member it describes?
Write the name of the correct person in the banner.

He was the final prophet of Allah ﷻ. He was born
in Makkah. Allah gave him His final book, the Qur'an

She was a business woman. She was a beautiful
noble woman. She married Muhammad ﷺ.

She was the second oldest daughter
of Muhammad ﷺ and Khadijah ؓ.

She was younger than the two older daughters
of Muhammad ﷺ and older than Fatimah ؓ.

She was the oldest daughter of
Muhammad ﷺ.

In the Cave of Hira

 Tune in! The Cave of Hira is in the Mountain of Light near Makkah.
It is a very special cave.
Why?

Let us find out what *"special event"*
happened there.

Khadijah was a very kind woman.
Muhammad liked to help people
and Khadijah liked to make her husband happy.
So they gave much of their money to poor people.

They also helped many slaves to become free.
Slaves are people who are owned by other people.
They have to work without getting paid.
Many people who owned slaves in Makkah treated them badly.

Muhammad didn't like how the people of Makkah behaved.
He also did not believe in their gods and idols.
He wanted to know who the real God was.

Bilal was one of the slaves in Makkah.
Prophet Muhammad bought his freedom from his owner.
Bilal had a beautiful voice.
He became the first Mu'addin
to call people for *Salah* and
give the call of *Adhan*.
Bilal's parents were originally from Africa.
Bilal always stayed close to Rasulullah.

He started going to a cave to think and be alone.
The cave was high on top of a mountain.
That cave is called the Cave of Hira.
There was peace and quite in the cave.
Muhammad ﷺ would stay in the cave thinking for many days.
Khadijah ؓ would bring food and water to the cave.

Muhammad ﷺ wanted to know the truth about life. He wanted to know who has created us. He wanted to find out why we were created. He wanted to help his people to be good, but he did not know how to.

Do we know these words?

Rich
Worship
Slaves
Quite
Peace
Truth

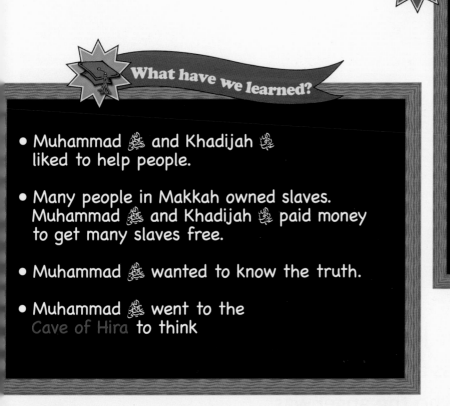

What have we learned?

- Muhammad ﷺ and Khadijah ؓ liked to help people.

- Many people in Makkah owned slaves. Muhammad ﷺ and Khadijah ؓ paid money to get many slaves free.

- Muhammad ﷺ wanted to know the truth.

- Muhammad ﷺ went to the Cave of Hira to think

OUR PROPHET • BOOK ONE

Lesson 14 — Angel Jibril visits Muhammad

Tune in!

The First Ayah in Arabic

اقْرَأْ بِاسْمِ رَبِّكَ الَّذِى خَلَقَ

"Read in the name of your Lord…."

This was the first ayah of the Qur'an revealed to Prophet Muhammad ﷺ.

Let us learn more about the Qur'an in this lesson!

One night, Muhammad ﷺ was in the Cave of Hira.
The dark cave became filled with light.
In the light, Muhammad ﷺ saw an angel.
It was Angel Jibril.

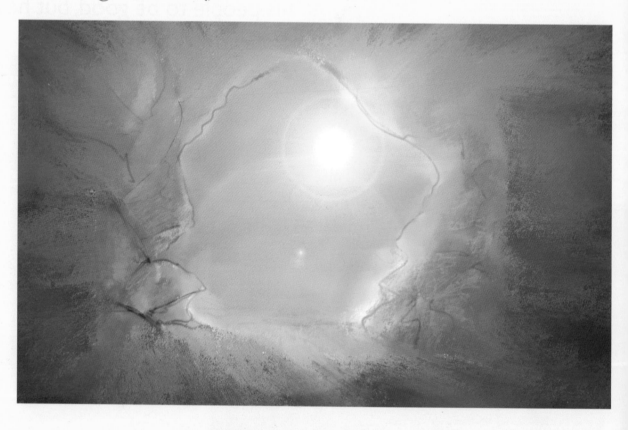

Allah sent Angel Jibril to Muhammad ﷺ.
Muhammad ﷺ was afraid.
He did not know who the angel was.

The Angel Jibril عليه السلام came close to Muhammad ﷺ and said,

Read!

I don't know how to read,

Muhammad ﷺ said.

Again Angel Jibril عليه السلام said,

Read!

But I don't know how to read,

Muhammad ﷺ said.

Jibril عليه السلام pressed him closer and said:

Read in the name of your Lord,
who made human beings from a clot of blood.
Read!
And your Lord is the most generous.
He taught human beings how to write with the pen.
He taught human beings what they did not know.

(Al-Alaq 96:1-5)

Muhammad ﷺ repeated these words.
Then the Angel Jibril عليه السلام left him.

Lesson 14

Muhammad ﷺ found himself alone in the cave.
He was still afraid. **Who was that visitor?** he wondered.

How did he get here?
What did he want from me?
What do his words mean?

What have we learned?

- One night, Angel Jibril ﷺ came to the cave of Hira.

- The Angel ﷺ brought Allah's message to Muhammad ﷺ

- Muhammad ﷺ was very scared.

Do we know these words?

Jibril
Clot
Generous
Wondered

Think about it!

CAUSE and EFFECT

Muhammad ﷺ was in the Cave of Hira
when he received the first *Wahy* from Allah ﷻ.
Why did Muhammad ﷺ go to the Cave of Hira?
Write the "causes" in the diagram below.

▶....CAUSE.1....

He wanted to find
out about
the true Creator

▶....CAUSE.2....

▶....EFFECT.....

Prophet Muhammad ﷺ
left his home
to pray and think
in the Cave of Hira.

▶....CAUSE.3...

▶....CAUSE.4....

Lesson 15 Khadijah Comforts Muhammad

Tune in!

Waraqah, the wise cousin of Khadijah

Prophet Muhammad was scared
after his first meeting with Angel Jibril.

He went home and Khadijah comforted him.
Then Khadijah took him to see her wise old cousin, Waraqah.
What did Waraqah say?

Let us find out in this lesson!

Muhammad came down
from the Cave of Hira.
He went back to his home.
He was frightened.

On the way he saw Angel Jibril
standing in the sky.
Everywhere Muhammad
turned there was the angel!

Angel Jibril said,

*"Muhammad!
You are Allah's messenger
and I am Jibril."*

The angel then disappeared.

Angel Jibril is one of the
archangels of Allah.
An archangel is a very
important angel.
Angel Jibril brought Allah's
messages to all the prophets.
We believe in the angels of Allah.

Muhammad ﷺ reached home.
Khadijah ﵂ saw that he was distressed.
> *"Cover me up! Cover me up!"*

Muhammad ﷺ said,
> *"I am afraid. I have seen such a strange thing."*

Then Muhammad ﷺ told Khadijah ﵂
what had happened in the cave.
Khadijah ﵂ comforted him. She said to him
> *"Do not be afraid. You are an honest and truthful man.*
> *You are kind to everyone. You help the poor.*
> *Allah loves people like you. He will take care of you."*

Khadijah ﵂ had a cousin named Waraqah.
He was a wise old man.
He was a pious Christian.
He knew about prophets who came before: Ibrahim, Musa and 'Isa ﵇.
He had read and believed in the books that were sent by Allah.

Muhammad ﷺ and Khadijah ﵂ went to Waraqah.
They told him what happened in the cave.
Waraqah said,
> *"The person who came to you was an angel.*
> *Allah sends this angel to the prophets.*
> *Allah has chosen you, O Muhammad, to be His prophet."*

He said,

*"Some of the people will become your enemies.
I am afraid they will try to hurt you."*

Prophet Muhammad ﷺ asked.

*"Why will they hurt me?
Why will they become my enemies?"*

Waraqah replied,

*"When a prophet teaches the truth, some people don't like it.
Many people don't like to change their bad behavior.
Most people don't like to change their wrong beliefs.
They get angry when a prophet tries to correct them."*

Muhammad ﷺ and Khadijah رضى الله عنها thought about this.
They did not know what would happen next.

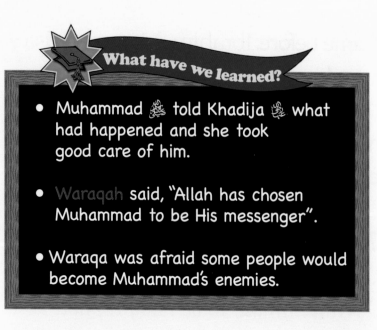

What have we learned?

- Muhammad ﷺ told Khadija رضى الله عنها what had happened and she took good care of him.

- Waraqah said, "Allah has chosen Muhammad to be His messenger".

- Waraqa was afraid some people would become Muhammad's enemies.

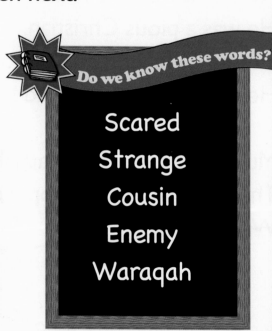

Do we know these words?

Scared
Strange
Cousin
Enemy
Waraqah

52

Muhammad ﷺ Becomes Rasulullah

Lesson 16

Prophet Muhammad ﷺ, Allah's Rasul

Who is Rasulullah?
What does Allah want a *Rasul* to do?
Who was the first *Rasul* of Allah?

Tune in!

Let us find out in this lesson!

Angel Jibril ﷺ came again.
He brought Muhammad ﷺ more messages from Allah.

Angel Jibril ﷺ said,

"Do not be afraid!
Allah has chosen you to be His prophet and messenger.
You are now Rasulullah, the Messenger of Allah
You will teach Islam to the world.
Allah will give you the Qur'an.
The Qur'an is Allah's last book."

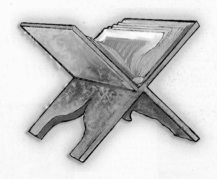

Lesson 16

He said,

"I will teach you the Qur'an.
Then you will teach the Qur'an to everyone.
Believers in Islam will be called Muslims."
The disbelievers will be called Kuffar.
The Kuffar are those who don't believe in God,
His messenger and the day of Qiyamah.

Muhammad ﷺ asked,

"How will I teach Islam?"

Angel Jibr'il عليه السلام said,

"You will stand up and tell people to believe in one God, Allah.
He made everything and everyone. Nothing is like Him.
He has no father, mother, sons or daughters.
One day everything will end.
That day is called the Qiyamah.
Tell the people that everyone will die.
But the dead will come back to life again.
They will be rewarded for their good deeds.
They will be punished for their bad deeds."

Muhammad ﷺ said,

"O Allah! I will do what You want me to do.
I will teach the people about Islam."

What have we learned?

- Angel Jibril عليه السلام told Muhammad ﷺ, "You are now Rasulullah."

- Allah سبحانه وتعالى told Muhammad ﷺ to teach Islam.

- Allah سبحانه وتعالى will reward the good people and punish the bad people.

Do we know these words?

Afraid
Rasulullah
Teach
Reward
Punishment

Allah rewards good deeds • Allah rewards good deeds •

55

Rasulullah ﷺ Teaches his Family and Friends

Lesson 17

Tune in!

The First Muslims

Allah ﷻ says in the Qur'an:

*"And the people who are first in accepting Islam
are the nearest to Allah in the Garden of Happiness."*
(Al-Waqi'ah: 10–12)

Let us read about the very first Muslims!

Rasulullah ﷺ talked to his family and friends about Islam first.
He told them:

"Allah has made me Rasulullah.
I am His prophet and messenger.
I will teach you the religion of Islam.
I will teach you Allah's book, the Qur'an.
I will teach you what is right.
I will tell you what is wrong
so that you stay away from it."

The First Muslims to accept Islam were:

Khadijah ﵂ , Ali ﵁, Abu Bakr ﵁, and Zaid ﵁

Lesson
17

His wife Khadijah said,

You are honest.
You are a good husband.
I believe that you are Rasulullah.

You are a man everyone trusts.
You are a good cousin to me.
I believe that you are Rasulullah

said his young cousin 'Ali .

His servant Zaid said,

You are a kind man.
You are a good master.
I believe that you are Rasulullah.

You always tell the truth.
You are a good friend too.
I believe that you are Rasulullah

said his best friend Abu Bakr .

Other people who knew Rasulullah
said they believed in him.
They also became Muslims.

Lesson 17

A Muslim who saw Rasulullah is called a *Sahabi*. This means "friend" or "companion."

When we hear the name of a *Sahabi*, we say,

"Radi Allahu anhu."

This means:

"May Allah, the Highest, be pleased with him or her."

An Arabic after the name of a *Sahabi*

reminds us to say, *"Radi Allahu anhu."*

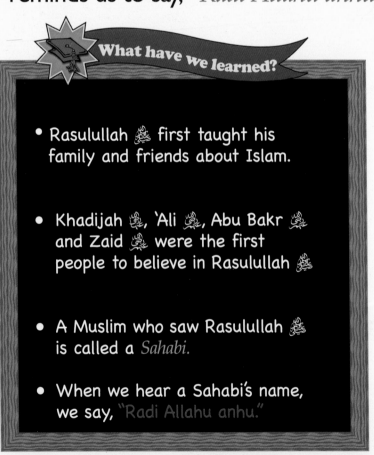

What have we learned?

- Rasulullah ﷺ first taught his family and friends about Islam.

- Khadijah ﷺ, 'Ali ﷺ, Abu Bakr ﷺ and Zaid ﷺ were the first people to believe in Rasulullah ﷺ

- A Muslim who saw Rasulullah ﷺ is called a *Sahabi*.

- When we hear a Sahabi's name, we say, *"Radi Allahu anhu."*

Do we know these words?

Friend
Husband
Cousin
Sahabi
Remind

SIMILARITIES & DIFFERENCES

In this lesson we have read about
four very close *Sahabah* of Rasulullah ﷺ.
In the chart below write the
similarities and differences among these *Sahabah*.

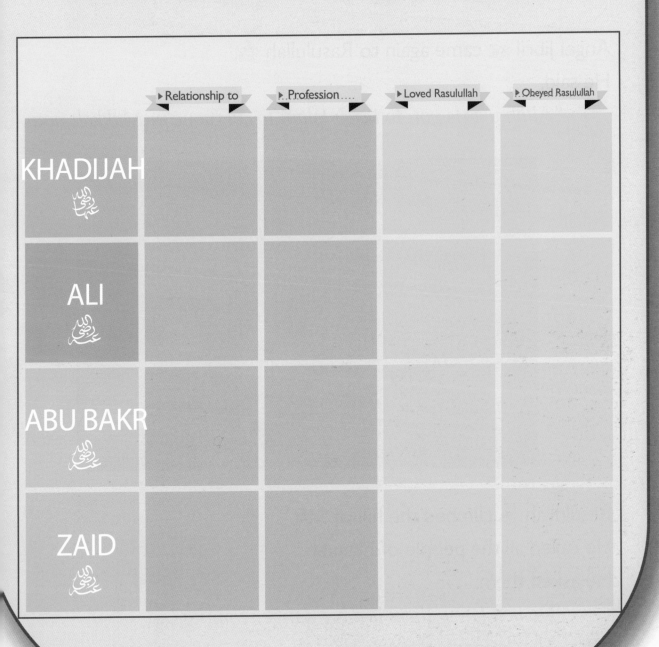

	▶ Relationship to ◀	▶ Profession ◀	▶ Loved Rasulullah ◀	▶ Obeyed Rasulullah ◀
KHADIJAH رضي الله عنها				
ALI رضي الله عنه				
ABU BAKR رضي الله عنه				
ZAID رضي الله عنه				

Rasulullah ﷺ Invites the People of Makkah

Tune in!

The Message of Islam

Prophet Muhammad ﷺ was the Messenger of Allah.
Allah asked him to give His Message to every one.
Rasulullah ﷺ did what Allah ﷻ had asked him to do.

Let us find out how he did it.

Angel Jibril ﷺ came again to Rasulullah ﷺ.
He said,

"Allah wants you to teach Islam to everyone in Makkah now."

"Do you know a danger is coming...."

Rasulullah ﷺ climbed the hill of Safa.
He called all the people of Makkah.
He asked them,

"Do you know there is a big danger coming?
The danger is very close.
You must do something about it right away."

The people of Makkah said,

"O Muhammad! We trust you.
You are as-Sadiq, the Truthful.
You are al-Amin, someone we can trust.
Tell us, what is this great danger."

Rasulullah ﷺ then told them what the danger was.
He told them they had to stop praying to many gods.
He told them to believe in Allah and obey Him.

Most of the people of Makkah were angry when they heard this.
They did not like what he was saying.
They did not believe him. They just turned away.

Rasulullah ﷺ spoke again, saying:

"Allah has made me His Rasul. I am Allah's prophet.
He has told me to teach you Islam. He has told me
to teach you His book, the Qur'an!

There is no god but Allah.

There is no one like Allah.

Allah made everything.

Rasulullah ﷺ told the people of Makkah that:

Everyone will die but Allah.

There is a Day of Qiyama, a Day of Judgment.

Everyone will come back to life again.

On that day, Allah will reward us for our good deeds and punish us for our bad deeds

Most of the people of Makkah did not want to listen to any of this.
They loved their gods and their idols.
They liked their wrong ways of doing things.
They told Rasulullah ﷺ:

> *"Is this what you called us here for?*
> *You say there is only One God.*
> *That is a silly idea!*
> *Our fathers and mothers prayed*
> *to many gods. This is our religion.*
> *We will not listen to what you say.*
> *We will never accept your religion."*

One of the people of Makkah who did not listen to Rasulullah ﷺ and who gave him a lot of trouble was Abu Lahab. Abu Lahab was an uncle of Rasulullah ﷺ. Allah ﷻ talkes about him in *Surah* Lahab .

(You can read the *Surah* in the book "Short Surahs").

They were very angry at Rasulullah ﷺ.
One by one they went to their homes.
A few people stayed and listened
to the message.
They believed in Rasulullah ﷺ.

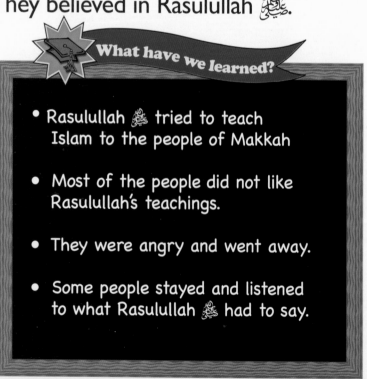

What have we learned?

- Rasulullah ﷺ tried to teach Islam to the people of Makkah

- Most of the people did not like Rasulullah's teachings.

- They were angry and went away.

- Some people stayed and listened to what Rasulullah ﷺ had to say.

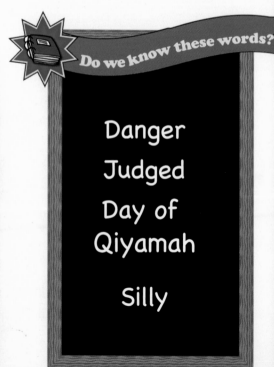

Do we know these words?

Danger

Judged

Day of Qiyamah

Silly

The Muslims and the Kuffar

Not everyone was happy with the message of Islam.
There were many people who tried to stop Rasulullah ﷺ
from teaching people to believe in Allah and do good deeds.

Let's read about them in this lesson.

Rasulullah ﷺ taught Islam to everyone who listened.

He taught them the words of the Qur'an.

He taught them to do good deeds.

He taught them to pray only to Allah.

More and more people in Makkah came to Rasulullah ﷺ.

They listened to him.

They listened to the words of the Qur'an.

They learned good things from him.

They believed in him.

They became Muslims.

They became the *Sahabah* of Rasulullah ﷺ.

The Revelation of the Quran

Angel Jibril came and recited parts of the Qur'an to Rasulullah ﷺ

Rasulullah ﷺ recited those *Ayahs* to Muslims.

People learned the *Ayahs* by heart. Some people wrote them on:

leaves

the bark
of trees

and clay plates.

The whole Qur'an was revealed over **23** years.

Lesson 19

Still, many people in Makkah did not like Rasulullah ﷺ.

They did not want to see or listen to him.

They did not want to hear the Qur'an.

These people were called the *Kuffar*.

The *Kuffar* did not believe in Allah.

They worshipped idols and images made by human beings.

They did not trust the message of Rasulullah ﷺ.

They did not like teaching of Islam.

They became enemies of Islam and Muslims.

Allah ﷻ was not happy with the *Kuffar*.

What have we learned?

- The Sahabah learned good things from Rasulullah ﷺ

- The Kuffar did not believe in Allah's message.

- Allah ﷻ was not happy with the Kuffar.

Do we know these words?

Stubborn

Kuffar

Revelation

The Kuffar Persecute the Muslims

Have you ever tried to be patient when some one was trying to make fun of you or hurt you? Allah likes a person who is patient and tolerant.

Let us read about the patience and tolerance of Rasulullah ﷺ and his early Sahabah.

There were not many Muslims in Makkah
but there were a lot of *Kuffar.*
Most of the *Kuffar* were rich and strong.
They became Rasulullah's ﷺ enemies.
They told him not to teach Islam.

They laughed at him when he talked.
They made fun of him when he walked

Some threw garbage on him.

Some tried to hurt him.

Some even tried to kill him.

Rasulullah ﷺ never said anything bad back to them.
He was patient.
He knew Allah ﷻ was helping him.
So he kept on teaching.

Most of the *Sahabah* were weak or poor.
Some of them were slaves.
Some of them were orphans.
Some of them were widows.
Some of them were young people.

The Kuffar persecuted the poor helpless Muslims.

They put them in chains
and dragged them
through the street.

They made them
lie in the hot sand.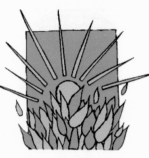

They made them
sit on burning coals.

They kept them
without food and water.

But the Muslims were brave. Their faith remained strong.

Rasulullah ﷺ told some of the Muslims to move to a land called Ethiopia.

Ethiopia had a good king. The king was a Christian.

Because he believed in One God too,

he protected the Muslims from the *Kuffar*.

GeoLink!

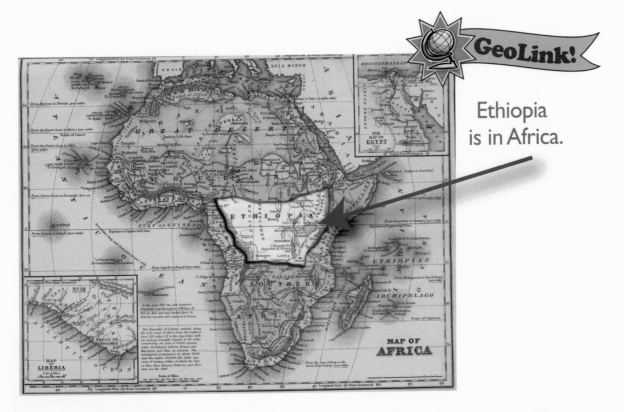

Ethiopia is in Africa.

What have we learned?

- The Kuffar made fun of Rasulullah ﷺ and tried to hurt him.

- The Kuffar persecuted the Muslims.

- Some Muslims moved to Ethiopia.

Do we know these words?

Dragged
Faith
Patient
Persecute
Protect
Suffer

The Lady Who Threw Grabage

Think about it!

There were many people who did not want to 👂 to Rasulullah ﷺ.
listen

They would do anything to hurt Rasulullah ﷺ and his *Sahabah*.

There was one lady who did not believe in Allah's words.

She did not like Muhammad ﷺ. She wanted to hurt him.

Everyday Rasulullah ﷺ would pass by her house and everyday

she brought a big pile of 🗑️ to her high window and dumped it on Rasulullah ﷺ.
garbage

Sometimes he would get hurt by the garbage. It made his clothes 👕
dirty.

He would go home and his body and his clothes.
wash

His young daughter, Fatimah ﷺ, was very sad when she saw her father hurt.

She helped him clean his clothes.

One day when Rasulullah ﷺ passed by the house of the woman she did not come out

to throw 🗑️ on him. It happened a few more times. Rasulullah ﷺ became worried
garbage

that something had happened to her. He went to her house and knocked at her 🚪

She asked him to come in. He found her very ill, lying on her bed. door.

"How are you feeling?" Rasulullah ﷺ asked,

"I did not see you for a few days so came to make sure that everything is all right."

The lady could not believe that the man whom she was giving so much trouble would

come to visit her when she was . She was ashamed of her behavior.
sick

She apologized for her mean acts. She told Rasulullah ﷺ,

"You are kind and *I was wrong."*
generous,

Rasulullah ﷺ forgave her and she began to cry. She apologized to Rasulullah ﷺ and said,

"You are definitely the messenger of Allah."

She passed away soon after, a believer in Allah and His Messenger.

Allah says :" Return evil with that which is best" (23:96)

Hijrah to Ethiopia

Tune in!

The Kuffar hurt and tortured the Muslims in Makkah.
Rasulullah ﷺ told the Muslims to
leave Makkah and move to another land.

Do you know where they went?

Most of the Kuffar were rich and strong.
The Muslims were not.
Rasulullah ﷺ advised some Muslims to leave Makkah.
He asked them to make *Hijra* to the land of Ethiopia.

Hijrah means *"to leave one place for another."*
A small group of Muslims quietly left Makkah for Africa.

GeoLink!

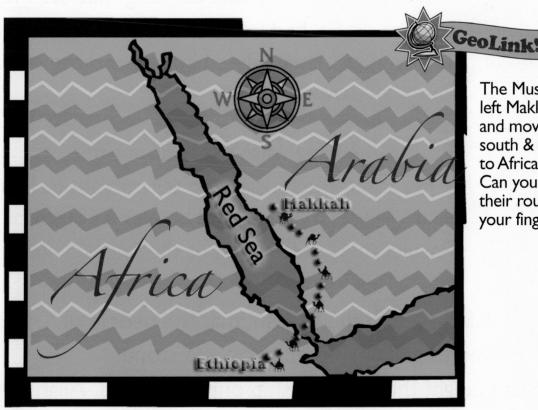

The Muslims
left Makkah
and moved
south & west
to Africa.
Can you trace
their route with
your finger.

Lesson 21

The King of Ethiopia was a good man.
His was called *Najashi*.
He was a Christian and he believed in
One God. Rasulullah ﷺ thought that he
would protect the Muslims.

The Kuffar found out that some of the
Muslims left. They were very angry.
Some of them followed the Muslims to Ethiopia.

They went to the palace of King *Naja*
They told the king that the Muslims
had left the religion of their fathers.
They asked him to hand the Muslims
over to them.

But the King wasn't sure about this.
He asked the Muslims to tell him about Islam.
Jafar ؓ was a *Sahabi* and he was a cousin of
Rasulullah ﷺ. He spoke to the *Najashi* about Islam

Jafar ؓ told the Najashi that the people of Arabia
prayed to gods made of wood and stone.
Islam taught them to worship only One God, Allah ﷻ.

Rasulullah ﷺ taught them to do good things.

He told the king that the Kuffar treated the Muslims harshly.

They were not happy with Islam.

After listening to Ja'far ﷺ, King *Najashi* told the Kuffar to go home.

He told them that the Muslims were welcome to live peacefully in his kingdom.

The king became friends with the Muslims.

Allah ﷻ says in the Qur'an:

"...The nearest among them in love to the believers you will find are those who say, we are christians'."

Al-Maidah 5:21

What have we learned?

• Many Muslims were persecuted and tortured by the Kuffar.

• Some Muslims moved to Ethiopia to live in peace there.

• The King of Ethiopia protected the Muslims from the Quraish and allowed them to live in his Kingdom.

Do we know these words?

Ethiopia

Africa

Ja'far

Najashi

Harshly

Lesson
21

We have learned about King Najashi of Ethiopia and about the Quraish of Makkah who were Kuffar. Below you can chart some of the differences and some of the similarities between them.

	▶ Difference #1	▶ Difference #2	▶ Difference #3	▶ Similarity #1
Quraish	.... to the Muslims.	Believed in	Did not listen to Rasulullah ﷺ	Had Power in Makkah
King Najashi	Kind to the Muslims.	Believed in	.... to Rasulullah ﷺ	Had Power in ....

The Teachings of Islam

Related to none,
Allah is One!
Equal to none.
No mother, no father,
No daughter or son,
Allah is One!
This is the most important teaching of Islam.

Let us learn more about this in this lesson!

Tune in!

The Kuffar could not stop Rasulullah ﷺ.
He kept teaching that:

There is no god but Allah

No one is like Him

He created everything

He has no daughter or son

He has no mother or father

The Kuffar turned away. They did not want to listen to this.

Lesson 22

But Rasulullah ﷺ kept teaching,

These idols are made of stone & wood.

They have no brains.

They are helpless.

They have no life.

Rasulullah ﷺ read the words of the Qur'an to the people. These words were about the Qiyamah, the Day of Judgment.

"When the sky will break

and the stars will fall,

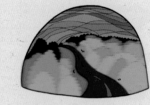

and the earth will shake,

and the mountains will fly into pieces...

on that day everything will end."

Rasulullah ﷺ taught the people of Makkah to do good and,

- Be kind to widows and orphans.
- Help the poor and those who need help.
- Respect and obey your parents.
- Be honest and fair.

Slowly more and more people in Makkah
started to think about Islam.
More people became Muslim.

The *Kuffar* became more and more angry.

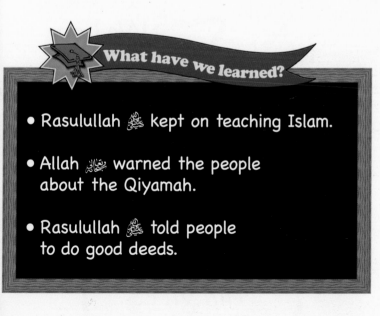

What have we learned?

- Rasulullah ﷺ kept on teaching Islam.

- Allah ﷻ warned the people about the Qiyamah.

- Rasulullah ﷺ told people to do good deeds.

Do we know these words?

Created

Partners

Heavens

Obey

Accept

The Kuffar Try to Bribe Rasulullah ﷺ

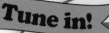

The Message of Islam

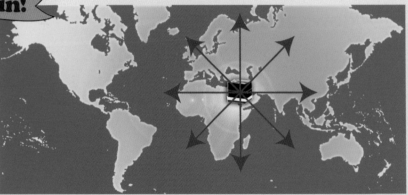

Al-Hamdulillah, there are more than one billion Muslims in the world today!
The population of Muslims has grown very fast since the time of Rasulullah ﷺ.

The growth of Muslims during the time of Rasulullah ﷺ
made the *Kuffar* of Makkah very nervous.
They tried to stop the spread of Islam in any way they could.

The Kuffar were angry because more and more people in Makkah were becoming Muslim. They said:

We have to find a way.

We have to stop Muhammad.

What does he want?

Maybe we can give it to him!

Some thought
he wanted
to be their king.

Some thought
he wanted
to be rich.

Some thought
he wanted
a beautiful wife.

One of the Kuffar said,

> *"We should give Muhammad anything he wants*
> *if he stops teaching people Islam. We must stop him*
> *from teaching the Qur'an."*

The Kuffar of Makkah went to Rasulullah's house. They said,

> *"Muhammad, we know you are a good man.*
> *We know you are **as-Sadiq** and **al-Amin**.*
> *But we do not like your religion, Islam. Do not say*
> *anything more against our gods.*
> *We will give you anything you want."*

They made Rasulullah ﷺ an offer. They told him,

> *"If you want power, we will make you our king.*
> *If you want money, we will make you very rich.*
> *If you want to marry a beautiful woman,*
> *we will get you one."*

Rasulullah ﷺ said,

*"I do not want power. I do not want money.
I do not want a beautiful wife.
All I want is that you believe in One God and do good works."
I want you to stop doing evil works.*

"I am Rasulullah," he said,

*"I am Allah's Prophet and Messenger. I do what Allah tells
me to do. And I will go on doing what Allah wants me to do."*

This answer made the *Kuffar* very angry.

They left Rasulullah's house. They met once again. One of them said,

*"We must try something else. We cannot scare him.
We cannot bribe him. And we cannot wait anymore.
Muhammad will become very strong.
More and more people will become Muslim."*

They talked more about this.

But they did no know what to do.

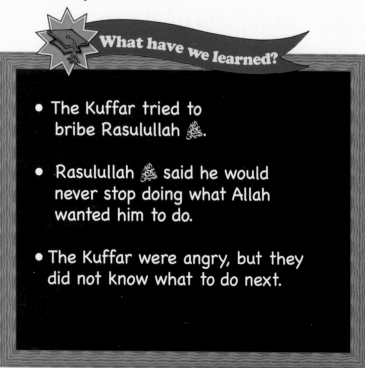

What have we learned?

- The Kuffar tried to bribe Rasulullah ﷺ.

- Rasulullah ﷺ said he would never stop doing what Allah wanted him to do.

- The Kuffar were angry, but they did not know what to do next.

Do we know these words?

Bribe

Beautiful

Wife

Offer

Rich

More and More People Accept Islam

Abu Dharr al-Ghiffari ﷺ,
Hamza ﷺ
and 'Umar ibn al-Khattab ﷺ.

What do these three men have in common?

Let us find out in this lesson!

Islam was growing in Makkah.

People outside Makkah began to hear about it too.

More and more people became Muslims.

More and more people learned the Qur'an.

Abu Dharr ﷺ came from a tribe called *Ghiffar*.

One day he met with Rasulullah ﷺ.

He liked Rasulullah ﷺ very much.

He liked what Rasulullah ﷺ was teaching.

Abu Dharr ﷺ said,

"O Muhammad! You really are Allah's prophet.
I accept Islam as my Faith."

Hamza ﷺ was one of Rasulullah's *uncles*.

Hamza ﷺ noticed the patience and peaceful manners of his nephew.

He was very impressed.

One day Hamza ﷺ went to Rasulullah ﷺ and said,

"Only a real prophet could behave as good as you do.
I accept Islam as my Faith."

'Umar did not like Muslims at first. He wanted to kill Rasulullah.

One day 'Umar heard some of the verses of the Qur'an.

'Umar said,

*"The Qur'an must be Allah's Book.
No human could write such beautiful words.
I accept Islam as my Faith."*

Many other people accepted Islam too.

The *Kuffar* of Makkah became very worried.

They were afraid of the teachings of Islam.

They decided to persecute Rasulullah and his family even more.

They told all the people of Makkah to stop talking to the Muslims.

They told the people to stop selling and buying anything from the

They even told the people to stop giving them food and water.

Story
Umar ﷜ Accepts Islam

The Kuffar were bothering the Muslims everyday.
One day Rasulallah ﷺ prayed,

"O Allah!
Help the Muslims by making one of these two men believe:
'Umar ibn al-Khattab or Abu Jahl ibn Hisham."

That same day 'Umar became very angry with the Muslims. He left his house with his sword, intending to kill Rasulullah ﷺ. On the way he met one of his friends who was secretly a Muslim. The man asked him, *"Where are you going 'Umar?"* Umar said,

"I am going to end this Islam business once and for all!
I am going to kill Muhammad!"

The man became very afraid. He did not want 'Umar to kill Rasulullah ﷺ. So he told 'Umar something to make him forget about the plan.

"How will you be safe from Muhammad's family,
the Bani Hashim" said the man, *"if you kill him?*
They will want revenge against you."

'Umar became angry and said,

"It sound likes you too are a Muslim!"

The man said,

"Forget about me.
Your own sister and her husband are Muslims."

'Umar was furious.
He walked to his sister's house and listened at the window.
He heard strange words coming from inside,
words he'd never heard before.
They were reading verses from the Qur'an.
He then started banging on the door.

"Let me in! Let me in!" he shouted.

Lesson 24

'Umar's sister and her husband became afraid.
They finally let 'Umar in.

"What were you two reading in here!" he demanded.

They said,

"Nothing. We were just talking."

'Umar said,

"Maybe you two have become Muslim!"

Then his brother-in-law said to him,

"What if all of our people's gods are not real 'Umar?"

When he heard these words 'Umar slapped him very hard.
His sister came to push him away from her husband and
'Umar hit her so hard her face began to bleed.

She was so upset by this she said,

*"Our people's gods are not real!
I witness that there is no god but Allah and
that Muhammad is His slave and His Messenger!*

When he saw his sister bleeding 'Umar felt bad.
He calmed down and said,

*"Give me the pages that you
were reading so I can read it too."*

His sister said to him,

*"You are not clean.
Only someone who has made wudu'
can touch these pages."*

'Umar then took a jug of water and made *wudu*'.
Then he took the writing and read what was on it.
It was *Surah Taha* of the Qur'an.
After he had finished reading 'Umar had tears in his eyes. He said,

"Take me to where Muhammad is."

Rasulullah was at home when 'Umar decided to look for him.
The Muslims who were with Rasulullah were worried when
they saw 'Umar at the door. They were afraid he was going to
make trouble. But Rasulullah told them not to fear.

'Umar asked to see Rasulullah. He went to the Prophet
and said,

"O Muhammad!
I believe that there is only One God, Allah.
I believe that you are certainly the Messenger of Allah."

In this way Rasulullah's *du'a* was answered.
'Umar ibn al-Khattab had embraced Islam.

What have we learned?

- More and more people became Muslims.

- Many people thought Rasulullah was a special man.

- More people became Sahabis.

- The Kuffar stopped talking to the Muslims.

Do we know these words?

Eternal

Firm

Tribe

Verses

Sahabah

The Boycott

Faith and Patience

Allah tests all of us with hardship and sadness at sometime in our lives. Since prophets were human beings, Allah tested them also with many difficulties and hardships.

Let us learn about some of the difficulties that Prophet Muhammad ﷺ experienced.

Many people in Arabia were becoming Muslim.
The *Kuffar* were worried.
They were afraid of the teachings of Islam.
They did not want to change their old ways.

The *Kuffar* decided to persecute the whole family of Rasulullah.
They decided to boycott Rasulullah ﷺ and the Muslims.

For three years, the Kuffar forced Rasulullah ﷺ, his family and other Muslims to live in a hot, dry valley near Makkah.

No one would talk to them. No one would sell them anything. The Muslims had almost no food and water.

But Rasulullah ﷺ and the Muslims were strong.
They had faith in Allah ﷻ.
They did not give up.

Finally the Kuffar let the Muslims come out of the valley.
They saw that they would not change their beliefs.

Rasulullah's wife Khadijah ؓ became sick.
His uncle, Abu Talib, grew old.
They became very sick because of the boycott.
Soon after the boycott ended, they passed away.

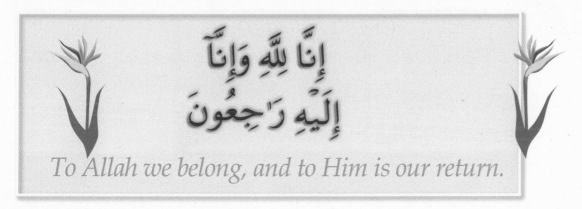

إِنَّا لِلَّهِ وَإِنَّا
إِلَيْهِ رَاجِعُونَ

To Allah we belong, and to Him is our return.

Rasulullah ﷺ was very sad when they died.
He loved them very much.
His uncle took care of him when he grew up.
Abu Talib loved Muhammad ﷺ like his own son.

Rasulullah ﷺ loved his wife Khadijah ؓ very much.
She believed in him and helped him when no one would listen.
She comforted him whenever he was worried.
He was very sad to lose her.

But Rasulullah ﷺ said,

"It was their time to leave this world.
Allah gives us life and He makes us die.
All of us will die one day. Only Allah lasts forever.
Only He is eternal and has no end."

Ali ؓ reported:
"I heard Rasulullah ﷺ say once that the best woman
in the world in her time was Maryam, daughter of 'Imran,
and the best woman in our time was Khadijah."
(Sahih Muslim)

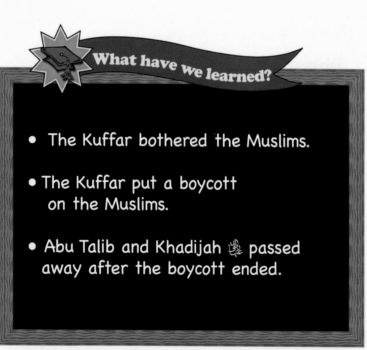

What have we learned?

- The Kuffar bothered the Muslims.

- The Kuffar put a boycott on the Muslims.

- Abu Talib and Khadijah ؓ passed away after the boycott ended.

Do we know these words?

Boycott

Valley

Comforted

Forever

The People of Tai'f

Lesson 26

Tune in!

The Town of Tai'f

The town of Tai'f is in Arabia.
Why did Prophet Muhammad ﷺ go there?
What happened to him there?

Let's find out!

After the death of his beloved uncle and his dear wife, Rasulullah ﷺ decided to travel to the town of Taif.

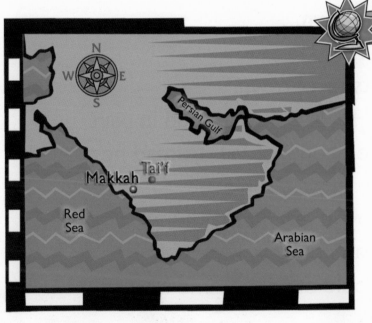

GeoLink!

Tai'f is a town to the east of Makkah. It is in the mountains. It had beautiful gardens and orchards. It does not get as hot in Taif as it does in Makkah. Can you find Taif?

Rasulullah ﷺ wanted to teach Islam to the people of Taif. He wanted to recite the Qur'an to them. He wanted them to become Muslims.

The people of Taif were rich and powerful.
They believed in many gods.
They did not like the teachings of Islam.
They did not want to hear the words of the Qur'an.

The people did not like what Rasulullah ﷺ said.
They all laughed when they heard him.
They made fun of him and said he was crazy.
Their children threw rocks at him.
They chased him out of the town.

Rasulullah ﷺ sat down outside of town.
He was hurt by the rocks. He was bleeding and in pain.
But he was not angry at the people of Taif. Instead he prayed.
He asked Allah ﷻ to guide these people.
He asked that Allah ﷻ show them the Truth.
Allah ﷻ accepted Rasulullah's prayers.
A few years later all the people of Taif became Muslim!

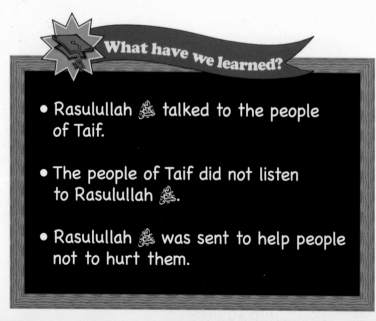

What have we learned?

- Rasulullah ﷺ talked to the people of Taif.

- The people of Taif did not listen to Rasulullah ﷺ.

- Rasulullah ﷺ was sent to help people not to hurt them.

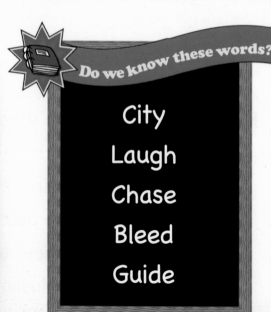

Do we know these words?

City
Laugh
Chase
Bleed
Guide

Lesson 26

Think about it!

CAUSE and EFFECT

Rasulullah ﷺ was sent as *Rahmatu lil'Alamin*,
a *"Mercy to the Worlds"*. His kindness has made
people love him and Islam.
Write the "effects" of Rasullullah's kindess below.
The first one has been done for you!

▸...CAUSE.....

Rasulullah ﷺ worked
for Khadijah ﷺ.
Her servant, Maisarah,
told her that Rasulullah ﷺ
was a good man.

▸...EFFECT.....

Khadijah ﷺ liked his honesty
and kindness.
She asked Rasulullah ﷺ to marry her.

▸...CAUSE.....

Prophet Muhammad ﷺ invited
his closest family and friends
to tell them about Islam.
His servant Zaid said,
"you are a kind and good master"

▸...EFFECT.....

▸...CAUSE.....

The people of Taif hurt him
and chased him out of the city.
Rasulullah ﷺ did not get angry
but prayed to Allah ﷻ to
guide them to Islam.

▸...EFFECT.....

Isra' and Miraj

The Night journey

بِسْمِ اللهِ الرَّحْمٰنِ الرَّحِيمِ

سُبْحَانَ ٱلَّذِىٓ أَسْرَىٰ بِعَبْدِهِۦ لَيْلًا مِّنَ ٱلْمَسْجِدِ ٱلْحَرَامِ

إِلَى ٱلْمَسْجِدِ ٱلْأَقْصَا ٱلَّذِى بَٰرَكْنَا حَوْلَهُۥ لِنُرِيَهُۥ مِنْ ءَايَٰتِنَآ

إِنَّهُۥ هُوَ ٱلسَّمِيعُ ٱلْبَصِيرُ ﴿١﴾

*"Glory to the One Who took His servant for a journey by night
from Masjid al–Haram to the Masjid al-Aqsa,
whose boundaries We did bless, in order that
We might show him some of Our signs:
for He is the One Who hears and sees all."*
(Al-Isra': 1)

Let us find out about Rasulullah's Night Journey!

Allah ﷾ knew how much Rasulullah ﷺ was suffering.
He knew how much the Muslims were hurting.
Rasulullah ﷺ and his *Sahabah* were very patient.
They had their complete trust in Allah ﷾.

Allah ﷾ decided to give Rasulullah ﷺ a great blessing.
He invited His dear Prophet ﷺ on the Isra' and Mi'raj.
Allah ﷾ wanted to show him *Jannah* (Heaven) and *Jahannam* (Hell).
So that he would tell people the pleasures of *Jannah* and
the panishments of *Jahannam*.
Allah ﷾ also wanted to honor Rasulullah ﷺ by talking directly to him

Allah ﷻ sent Angel Jibril ﷺ to bring Rasulullah ﷺ to *Heaven*.

Angel Jibril brought a Buraq for Rasulullah ﷺ to ride.

A Buraq was a creature from *Jannah*.

It was like a horse with wings.

The Buraq was able to travel very, very fast.

It could move in a flash of light from this world to *Heaven*.

First, Rasulullah ﷺ rode the Buraq to the city of Jerusalem.

They arrived in the blink of an eye.

This city was almost 800 miles from Makkah!

GeoLink!

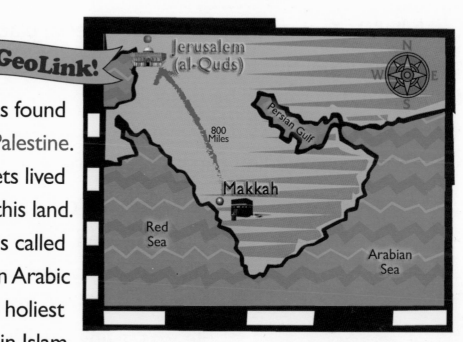

Jerusalem was found in a land called Palestine. Many prophets lived and taught in this land. Jerusalem is called *al-Quds* in Arabic This is the third holiest place in Islam.

Rasulullah ﷺ went to the Masjid al-Aqsa.

It is a very special place.

This part of his journey is called *Isra.*

There he saw all the prophets throughout history. Rasulullah ﷺ led them all in prayer.

Lesson 27

From here Rasulullah ﷺ went to *Jannah*.
This journey is called the **Mi'raj**.
He traveled with Angel Jibril.
He saw how beautiful *Jannah* is.
He prayed to Allah ﷻ to give *Jannah* to his *Ummah*.

Then he saw the terrible *Jahannam*.
It was a terrible place.
It was the Hellfire.
He prayed that Allah save his *Ummah*
from this place.

Rasulullullah ﷺ then came to a very special place.
It was called the *Sidrat ul-Muntaha*.
It is a place that cannot be described.
No creatures can pass the *Sidrat ul-Muntaha*.
No human, angel or jinn can go past here.

Three Muslims in prayer

But Allah ﷻ called Rasulullah ﷺ
and he passed *Sidrat ul-Muntaha*.
Allah spoke to him directly.
Allah ﷻ told the Prophet ﷺ that
He was giving the Muslims a special gift

That gift was *Salah*,
the five daily prayers.
By making *Salah* Muslims can
meet with Allah everyday.

After speaking to Allah ﷻ Rasulullah ﷺ
went back to his home in Makkah.
He found that his bed was still warm.
Though he traveled so far, his trip took only seconds.
The **Isra'** and **Mi'raj** was a great miracle!

The next day the Muslims learned about
Rasulullah's journey to Heaven.
They were happy to learn about his travels.

The Muslims thanked Allah ﷻ for honoring their prophet.
The Muslims thanked Allah ﷻ for the gift of *Salah.*
They thanked Allah ﷻ for the gift of the Qur'an,
and for the promise of Heaven.

Let us also thank Allah ﷻ for all
of His gifts and say *Al-Hamdu-lillah!*

What have we learned?

- Rasulullah ﷺ went to Al-Quds
  and then went up to Heaven.

- Rasulullah's journey from
  Makkah to Al-Quds is called Isra'.

- Rasulullah's journey from
  al-Quds to Heaven is called Mi'raj.

- He saw Jannah and Jahannam.

- Allah ﷻ gave Rasulullah ﷺ
  the gift of Salah.

Do we know these words?

Isra'

Miraj

Salat

Miracle

Jannah

Jahannam

The People of Madinah Accept Islam

Lesson 28

Tune in!

Madinah

Have you ever heard of a city called Madinah?
It is the city where Rasulullah ﷺ
and the *Sahabah* built the Masjid al-Nabawi.

Let us find out more about the people of Madinah!

For thirteen years, Rasulullah ﷺ invited
the people of Makkah to come to Islam.
But most of the leaders of Makkans did not accept Islam.

GeoLink!

Madinah was another
impotant city in Arabia.
It was called *Yathrib*
at that time.
Every year people
from all over Arabia
came to Makkah to
visit the Ka'bah.

Rasulullah ﷺ met with the people of
Madinah when they came to visit the Ka'bah.

He told them about Islam. They listened to him.

He told them that
there is only One God.

He told them that
Islam is the religion of Allah.

He told them that
the Qur'an is Allah's final Book.

He asked them to
stop worshipping idols.

He told them to obey Allah ﷻ and do good actions.
He told them to obey Allah ﷻ and avoid bad actions.
Rasulullah ﷺ recited the Qur'an to the Madinans.
They listened and then they said,

*"Islam is the religion of Allah.
The Qur'an is Allah's Book.
Muhammad is Allah's messenger and prophet.
We believe in Islam."*

Rasulullah ﷺ said to them,

*"Allah loves all of you. I love all of you.
You are now Allah's Ansar (His Helpers).
You are the helpers of Islam and the helpers of me."*

Lesson 28

The people from Madinah were very happy to hear this.
They were very happy to be the *Ansar* or helpers of Islam.
They said,   *"We believe in Allah.*
We believe in Rasulullah.
We are Muslims. We will be Allah's Ansar.
All Muslims are brothers and sisters.
We will do what Allah and Rasulullah tell us to do.
We will work for Islam."

They then went back to Madinah.
They told their people about Rasulullah ﷺ and Islam.

What have we learned?

- Rasulullah ﷺ taught Islam to some people from Madinah

- Many people in Madinah became Muslims.

- The Muslims from Madinah are called the Ansar, the Helpers.

Do we know these words?

Invited

Ansar

Share

Helper

Prophet Muhammad ﷺ The Peacemaker

Allah ﷻ gave Prophet Muhammad ﷺ great wisdom.
Rasulullah ﷺ did not like fighting.
He always tried to make peace between people.
They called him *the peace maker.*

Tune in!

Let us read one of the stories of when Prophet Muhammad ﷺ brought peace among the fighting tribes of Makkah.

Before Rasulullah ﷺ became a prophet,
he was known to be the most *trusted* person in Makkah.

The people of the town would ask him
to help them solve their arguments.
They knew that he would always be just and fair.

Once the Ka'bah was damaged by rain and flood. The tribe of Quraish worked long and hard to repair it. When the work was done they began to argue over who would place the famous Black Stone, the *al-Hajral-Aswad,* in the Ka'bah.

97

Lesson
29

The tribes were getting angry with each other.
One person suggested that they should ask what
they should do from the *next* person who came to the Ka'bah.
Everyone agreed on this suggestion.

Young Muhammad ﷺ was the next person that came to the Ka'bah
Everyone was happy to see him.
They shouted, *"As-Sadiq is coming!"* and *"al-Amin is coming!"*

They told Muhammad ﷺ the problem and
asked him to help them solve it.
Muhammad ﷺ took a little time to think of a solution.

Then he asked for a large piece of strong cloth.
He spread the cloth on the ground next to the Ka'bah.

He picked up the Black Stone and put it in the middle of the cloth
Then he asked the leader of each tribe to take hold of the cloth.
Together all the leaders lifted the cloth and the stone.
Muhammad ﷺ then picked the stone gently
and placed it carefully into the wall of the Ka'bah.

Every one was happy.

Every one got a chance to help place the *Hajr al-Aswad* in its place.

No one was left out.

It was a simple and fair solution.

Only Muhammad ﷺ thought of it!

He hated wars and disputes.

He wanted all people to live in peace which each other.

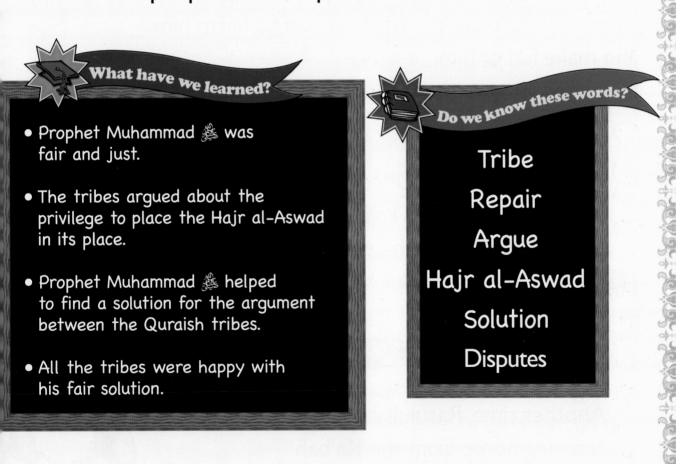

What have we learned?

- Prophet Muhammad ﷺ was fair and just.

- The tribes argued about the privilege to place the Hajr al-Aswad in its place.

- Prophet Muhammad ﷺ helped to find a solution for the argument between the Quraish tribes.

- All the tribes were happy with his fair solution.

Do we know these words?

Tribe

Repair

Argue

Hajr al-Aswad

Solution

Disputes

Lesson 30

Kindness and Compassion

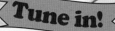

Tune in!

If someone tried to hurt you or make fun of you,
what would you do to that person?
What would you tell him or her?

**Let us find out what Rasulullah ﷺ
used to do in such situations.**

Muhammad ﷺ is the Messenger of Allah ﷻ.
He was loving and kind to everyone he met.
But there were people who wanted to harm him
and make fun of him.
He always forgave them and prayed for them.

Once when he was passing by a street
a *kafir* woman tried to make him angry.
She thew garbage on Rasulullah ﷺ.
But he did not get angry at the woman.

Another time, Rasulullah ﷺ was
coming home from the Ka'bah.
A man took mud in his hands and
threw it at his face. Rasulullah ﷺ
did not yell at the man.
He tried to clean as much mud
as he could and then he walked home.

His young daughter, Fatima ﵍, cried
when she saw her father covered with mud.
She cleaned the mud from her father's face and kept crying.
It gave her great pain to see her father being hurt.

Prophet Muhammad ﷺ told his daughter not to cry or worry.
He said that when you work for the cause of Allah ﷻ
He protects you from any harm.
Allah ﷻ teaches us to be always patient and thankful to Him.

Rasulullah ﷺ was
the *Messenger of Peace and Love.*
He was patient when people hurt him.
He always forgave those people.
In this way he showed those who
wanted to hurt him that he was different.
His kindness and compassion made many
of his enemies change their minds.
They became his friends and followers.

What have we learned?

- Prophet Muhammad ﷺ was very patient with his enemies.

- He never hurt anyone, not even those who tried to hurt him.

- His kindness and compassion made many of his enemies his friends and followers.

Do we know these words?

Harm

Worry

Kindness

Compassion

Lesson 31

Keeping Promises

Tune in!

Rasulullah ﷺ said:

"A person who does not keep his promises has no religion."
(Ibn al-Najjar)

Let us read and find out how our Prophet Muhammad ﷺ kept his promises!

Prophet Muhammad ﷺ was known as *Al-Amin,* a person you can trust.
Allah ﷻ taught us to keep our word and fulfill our promises.
Prophet Muhammad ﷺ was the greatest example of this.

One time Rasulullah ﷺ promised a man named 'Abdullah that he would meet him at a certain place. Rasulullah ﷺ kept his promise. He arrived at the place on time as they had agreed.

But the Prophet ﷺ did not find 'Abdullah there. So he sat and waited for him to come. But 'Abdullah did not come. He forgot about the meeting with Rasulullah ﷺ.

After three days, 'Abdullah remembered the meeting. He ran to the place where he had agreed to meet Rasulullah ﷺ. He found Prophet Muhammad ﷺ still sitting there waiting for him.

'Abdullah was surprised by the way the Prophet ﷺ kept his promise. Rasulullah ﷺ greated him with a smile and said *Assalamu Alaikum*. He said to himself that Rasulullah ﷺ was a very special person. He realized that it was important to keep one's promise.

Let's follow the *Sunnah* of our dear Prophet ﷺ. Let's always keep our promises.

What have we learned?

- Prophet Muhammad ﷺ always kept his promises.

- We should follow his *Sunnah* and always keep our promises.

- We must greet people with a smile.

- We must welcome them with Assalmu Aliakum.

Do we know these words?

Promise

Surprised

Realized

Sunnah

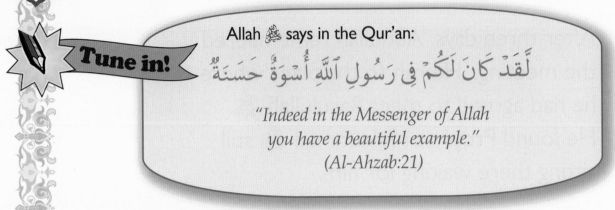

Lesson 32 The Teachings of Our Prophet ﷺ

Tune in!

Allah ﷻ says in the Qur'an:

لَّقَدْ كَانَ لَكُمْ فِي رَسُولِ ٱللَّهِ أُسْوَةٌ حَسَنَةٌ

*"Indeed in the Messenger of Allah
you have a beautiful example."*
(Al-Ahzab:21)

Rasulullah ﷺ taught us the *Qur'an.*

He showed us how to follow its teachings.

The *Qur'an* is the final revelation of Allah ﷻ.

The teachings of the Qur'an are for everyone.

The message of the Qur'an are for all times.

Rasulullah's actions are called the *Sunnah.*

Rasulullah ﷺ is the best model for us to follow.

The *Sahabah* and the early Muslims
wrote down the teachings of Rasulullah ﷺ.
These writings are called *Hadith.*
There are many books of *Hadith.*
Two of big books of *Hadith* are called
Sahih al-Bukhari and Sahih Muslim.

Let us learn one *Hadith* of Rasulullah now!

One day Rasulullah ﷺ said,

> *"Deeds are judged by intentions,*
> *and everyone will get the reward*
> *for what he or she intends…"*
>
> (Sahih al-Bukhari and Sahih Muslim)

Rasulullah ﷺ told us that our intentions are very important.
Allah ﷻ knows what is in our hearts and in our minds.

He gives us rewards for
our good intentions.
If we plan to do something
good and cannot do it,
Allah will be happy with us
for our good intentions.
We will still be rewarded
for our good intention.

Intentions are very important.
Allah ﷻ made it an important part of our worship.
When we make *Salah*, we must make the intention in our hearts.
We pray with the intention of getting Allah's pleasure.

Lesson
32

When we help the poor, needy or any human being we must make an intention of doing it for the sake of Allah. When we work hard to get good grades in school with the intention of getting smarter, Allah ﷻ will reward us for it.

Whenever we do some thing our intentions must always be to do good and avoid evil. We should never intend to harm or hurt anyone. We should always have the intention of helping all people and obeying Allah ﷻ

Do we know these words?

Intention
Pleasure
Charity
Knowledgeable

What have we learned?

• Allah ﷻ rewards us for our good intentions.

• We should always have good intentions.

• We should never intend to harm or hurt anyone.

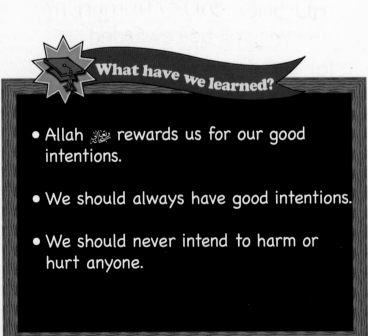

106

Unity in Diversity

LET'S GET TOGETHER

Come friends!
Let's get together.
We hold hands
And work together.
We can do many things better
When we stay close together.

Let's find out what Rasulullah ﷺ taught us about working together!

Tune in!

The Qur'an and the *Sunnah* tell us the truth of all human beings are one *Ummah*. They also teach us about special unity of the Muslim as one *Ummah* of Faith. *Ummah* means a community of people who have something in common. Islam teaches us that all human beings are one *Ummah* as all of them are created by One God and have common parents.

The Qur'an teaches us that all human beings one *Ummah*:

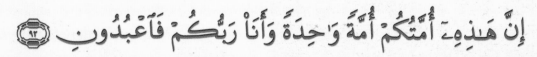

إِنَّ هَـٰذِهِۦ أُمَّتُكُمْ أُمَّةً وَاحِدَةً وَأَنَا۠ رَبُّكُمْ فَٱعْبُدُونِ ﴿٩٢﴾

"Verily, this Ummah of yours is a single Ummah and I am your Lord and Creator therefore worship Me alone.."

(al-Anbiya' 21:92)

Lesson 33

Allah ﷻ has also chosen Muslims as a special *Ummah* of Faith. The Muslim *Ummah* has a special mission, as the Qur'an says:

وَلْتَكُن مِّنكُمْ أُمَّةٌ يَدْعُونَ إِلَى ٱلْخَيْرِ وَيَأْمُرُونَ بِٱلْمَعْرُوفِ وَيَنْهَوْنَ عَنِ ٱلْمُنكَرِ ۚ وَأُوْلَٰٓئِكَ هُمُ ٱلْمُفْلِحُونَ ﴿١٤﴾

" Let there arise out of you an Ummah inviting to all that is good enjoining what is right, and forbidding what is wrong,: they are those who are successful.

(Al Imran 3:104)

Thus Muslims are special *Ummah* because they have a special mission. To succeed in any mission one needs both guidance and unity. Allah has provided Muslims guidance of the Qur'an and the *Sunnah* of Rasulullah ﷺ. Rasulullah ﷺ talked about Muslim unity:

"Allah is with the united community."

(al-Tirmidhi)

He also taught:

"The united community is blessed (by Allah)"

(Sunan Abi Da'ud)

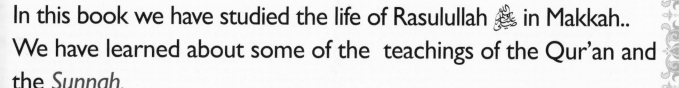

In this book we have studied the life of Rasulullah ﷺ in Makkah..
We have learned about some of the teachings of the Qur'an and the *Sunnah.*
We have also seen how they remained firm in their faith.
We have seen how patient they were when tortured..

We shall study in next volume the life of Rasulullah ﷺ in Madinah.
We shall read how a small Muslim community grew into large and united *Ummah.*
We shall see how Allah rewarded the Muslim *Ummah* for its faith and patience.

Let's follow the Qur'an and the *Sunnah.*
Let's work with our community to help everyone.

What have we learned?

- All humanity is one large community of Allah.

- Muslims are one Ummah of Faith with a special mission.

- We must practice and enjoin right and forbid what is wrong.

- We should be united and work together with every one for the common good.

Do we know these words?

Community

United

Benefit

Citizen